101
Secrets A Cool
Mom Knows

Sue Ellin Browder and Walter Browder
Illustrations by Walter Browder

RUTLEDGE HILL PRESS®

Nashville, Tennessee

A Division of Thomas Nelson, Inc.

www.ThomasNelson.com

Published by Rutledge Hill Press, a Division of Thomas Nelson,
Inc., P.O. Box 141000, Nashville, Tennessee, 37214.

Library of Congress Cataloging-in-Publication Data

Browder, Sue Ellin, 1946-
        101 secrets a cool mom knows / Sue Ellin Browder and
Walter Browder.
           p. cm.
        ISBN 1-4016-0135-9 (Hardcover)
1. Mothers-Life skills guides. 2. Parenting. 3. Mothers-Con-
duct of life.
    I. Title: One hundred and one secrets a cool mom knows.
II. Browder, Walter,   1939- III. Title.
    HQ759.B7594 2003
    649'.1--dc21
2002156111

Printed in the United States of America

05 06 07 08 09 — 5 4 3 2 1

With love and admiration for our cool moms,
Naoma Hurdle and Ruth Marie Browder,
who taught us "If it's to be, it's up to me"
and "Never despair. When life gets tough,
always remember: This, too, shall pass away."

Contents

Thanks!

Cool Moms always thank people who help and support them. So a great big thanks and a round of heartfelt applause go out to:

First of all, our adult offspring, Erin and Dustin, who were always eager as children to learn Cool Mom skills.

Then to Jennifer Browder, Michel Keet, Tom and Carol Brock, Liz O'Neil, Darlene and Durward Duffield, who gave us so much wonderful love and support. Also, to the Renaissance-Faire-costumed dad who taught us to hang spoons on our noses one Saturday at the Country Skillet in Willits, California. (Sorry, we lost your name. But we live in Willits now, so give us a call.)

And last, but far from least, to Larry Stone, Geoff Stone, Bryan Curtis, Jennifer Brett Greenstein, and all the other great players on the Rutledge Hill team.

Remember, kids, always say please and thank-you.

Introduction

As a mother today, you're as likely as any dad to teach your kids how to pitch a tent, kick a soccer ball, or fix a broken bicycle chain. In a phrase, you're what kids call a "Cool Mom." You know how to make things work. What's more, with the special insights you've learned from becoming strong and uniquely yourself, you're raising happier, more self-reliant, more confident children who know how to take on the world.

As a Cool Mom, chances are you've already taught your children lots of neat stuff to make them more capable and independent. But with your 24/7 schedule, you can always use extra help. That's why we wrote this book—to give you more Cool Mom secrets to pass along to the next generation.

What's a Cool Mom secret? It's a tidbit of knowledge or a special way of doing a job that produces big results with little effort. At the same time a child learns a handy skill (such as how to throw a spiral pass), a Cool Mom secret also teaches life's deeper lessons about perseverance, courage, honesty, and other character traits. Take hitting a baseball with the "sweet spot" of the bat, for example. As a child learns how to send that little white ball sailing high over the outfielders' heads, she's also learning it's not always those with the most raw power who succeed at what they set out to do. It's often those with the best insight.

Whistling with an acorn seems a simple skill. But while your kid is immersed in the fun of whistling with an old acorn, she's also learning some really important stuff (like how to persist, be patient, and develop a certain sensitive "touch" to solve problems). With just this one simple skill, you've taught her three (or more) character lessons without saying a word. And later in life, each time she uses the skill, the character lesson will automatically be recalled and reinforced. It's parallel learning at its best.

Cool Mom secrets are solutions that work. They go straight to the heart of whatever problem a child might be having and solve it quickly and effectively—no nonsense, no fuss. Any one of these secrets will leave a child feeling you've done something smart and cool. When a child is first learning to multiply, for example, anyone armed with Cool Mom Secret 17 can teach a kid how to multiply by nine in less than a minute. When a child wants to see a falling star, anyone who knows Cool Mom Secret 3, "How to 'Catch' a Falling Star," will know exactly how and where to find one.

Using Cool Mom secrets, you can teach a child how to fix a bicycle chain, how to see better in the dark, how to get a close-up look at a hummingbird, how to cruise on a skateboard, how to crack an egg with one hand, and even how to blow a six-foot soap bubble. Years later, whenever your kid uses any of these practical skills, he or she will proudly say, "My mom taught me that."

Now, is that cool, or what?

1. How to Use Chopsticks

Noodles are not only amusing but delicious.
　　　　　　　　—Julia Child, a Cool Mom of fine French cooking

A kid using chopsticks for the first time can be a pathetic sight: Noodles on her lap, sweet-and-sour sauce on her shirt, bits of meat zinging across the table like peas from a pea shooter.

Fortunately, you know how to come to your child's rescue. You know the high and complicated art of using chopsticks. With your help, she'll soon be delivering every bite directly into her mouth instead of her brother's lap. The secret lies in the way she holds the chopstick.

Of the several ways to hold chopsticks, here's the one easiest for a kid to learn. Since there are two chopsticks, let's call them Chopstick 1 and Chopstick 2.

First, have your child rest the fat (non-pointed) end of Chopstick 1 in the crotch of her thumb and forefinger, as shown in figure 1. Her thumb should clamp the fat end tight against her forefinger. Now have her lay the skinny (pointed) end of the stick across the end of her ring finger (as shown). Tell her to remember this: Chopstick 1 does not move. When she picks up food, Chopstick 1 remains stationary.

Second, have her grasp the fat end of Chopstick 2 between her thumb and forefinger, as shown. The end of her middle finger should be pressed tightly against Chopstick 2. She can

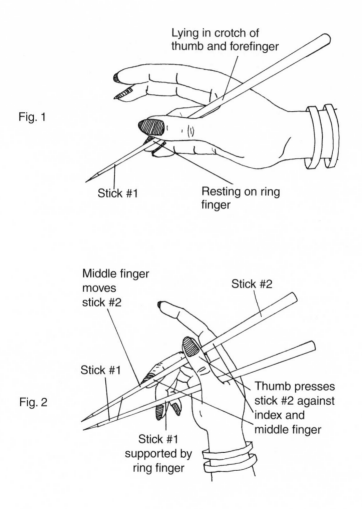

Fig. 1

Lying in crotch of thumb and forefinger

Stick #1

Resting on ring finger

Fig. 2

Middle finger moves stick #2

Stick #2

Stick #1

Thumb presses stick #2 against index and middle finger

Stick #1 supported by ring finger

now move Chopstick 2 by raising and lowering the end of her middle finger. When picking up food, it's Chopstick 2 that moves, and it's the middle finger that moves Chopstick 2.

Third, have her tap the pick-up tips against the table to even them up.

Now she's ready to pick up food. If she forgets, remind her again: Chopstick 2 moves. Chopstick 1 remains stationary.

As your child learns to use chopsticks, you can point out that eating politely seldom comes naturally. It takes practice, but it's worth learning. Unless, of course, you like noodles in your hair.

COOL MOM TIPS

- Square chopsticks are easier to use than round ones.
- Unfinished-wood chopsticks are easier to use than lacquered ones.
- Don't grasp chopsticks too tightly, or your hand will cramp.

2. How to Pick Up a Hamster

Friends gotta trust each other . . . 'cause ain't nothin' like a true friend.

—Mildred D. Taylor, Cool Mom of
Roll of Thunder, Hear My Cry

As a sign of affection, children want to pick up hamsters. But if a child picks up a hamster incorrectly, the tiny animal can be hurt. This can leave a child devastated and confused. How can loving a hamster possibly do it any harm?

But you know it's not *loving* the hamster that hurts. It's picking it up wrong. So teach your child how to pick up his hamster like a pet show judge. In this grip, the rodent's rump goes under the child's fingers and its head (and sharp teeth) go under the wrist.

Once the hamster is securely locked in place with the Pet Show Hamster Grip, it can't wriggle backward out of your child's hand, no matter how much it squirms.

Your kid can then place his free hand under the hamster and gently pick it up.

Wrapped in a cozy pocket of one hand above and the other below him, the hamster feels secure. Meanwhile your child's fingers, far from the animal's mouth, can never be nipped. Result: A warm-hearted relationship is born, one of mutual love, confidence, and trust.

As your child plays with his new pet, he's also learning one of life's little lessons: Establishing a warm bond with a new friend requires making sure the other guy feels cozy, comfortable, and secure.

COOL MOM FACTS

- The word *hamster* comes from the German verb hamstern, meaning to hoard or stow away.

- Hamsters have large cheek pouches that go all the way back to their shoulders.

- Hamsters will hibernate if the temperature gets low or there is little light.

- Hamsters are escape artists. They can squeeze through the tiniest opening, even the space between bars in most cages. So maybe your child should run a bed check on his hamster every night.

- A hamster can carry up to half its body weight in its cheek pouches. That would be like a ten-year-old child carrying thirty-seven to thirty-eight pounds of his belongings in his mouth.

3. How to "Catch" a Falling Star

Everything has its wonders, even darkness and silence.
—Helen Keller, Cool Mom of an inspirational life

To a child, a falling star looks like magic. As your child gazes raptly up into that coal-black, star-studded sky, all is silent and still. Suddenly, a bright fire streaks madly from zenith to horizon. Then it quietly vanishes forever. Unfortunately, because of light and air pollution, kids see precious few shooting stars anymore.

But that you can fix. You know a way your child can see hundreds, maybe thousands of falling stars in one night. They're as easy to catch as the 5:15 train home. Your child just has to be at a certain place at a certain time. During a meteor shower, she can catch them all.

Meteor showers (the remains of comets) appear on the same dates every year. When the Earth intercepts a comet's orbit, it rips through the debris the comet has left behind. These little bits of leftover comet (rocks and ice) zip through the Earth's atmosphere at six to forty-three miles per second, leaving behind fiery streaks. The result: a meteor shower. Several showers occur every year. But the two most spectacular are usually the Perseids (which show up on August 12) and the Leonids (which pass our little corner of the solar system on November 19). Both are as predictable as that 5:15 train.

The best time to watch shooting stars is between midnight and dawn. That's when the Earth has turned to face directly into the comet's path. So awaken your child shortly after midnight on August 12 or November 19 and head out to your preselected spot—any dark site with an open view of the sky. To find the best meteor-watching spots in your area, just call a telescope shop or the astronomy department at a local college. The meteor shower's name tells you where to look in the sky. The Leonid meteors come out of the constellation Leo. The Perseids come out of the constellation Perseus. Shortly after midnight on August 12, you'll find Perseus above and to the right of the North Star. On November 19, you'll find Leo high in the eastern sky.

If you live in a large city, stargazing can be doubly cool. That's because there are usually only a few good places to go see the display, and all the stargazers will be there. From midnight to dawn, a party atmosphere rules. To enjoy the show, you need only two reclining chairs and sleeping bags to protect you and your child from cold, dew, and maybe a few bugs.

How many meteors can you expect to see? Anywhere from one hundred to several thousand an hour. To find out this year's prediction, look in your local newspaper or an astronomy magazine like *Sky and Telescope* for the ZHR, or zenith hourly rate. That's the number of meteors you can expect to see in an hour.

You and your child will have a marvelous time lying in the dark, gazing up into the heavens, breathlessly waiting for the next fireball to streak across the sky. And as the shower ends, you'll come away feeling very close to one another, as people always do when they've just shared an awesome adventure.

4. How to Listen to Your Cat Talk

The more you talk to cats . . . the smarter they become. An occasional "nice kitty" will have no measurable effect; intelligent conversation is required.

—Lilian Jackson Braun,
Cool Mom of cat mysteries

A kid often wishes he knew what his cat is thinking. But the cat never says a word. So the child thinks the cat's thoughts must be locked forever behind those big, glow-in-the-dark eyes.

But, in fact, the cat is always "talking" without words, telling your child how it feels inside. The secret: Cats speak in what's called body language. They use their tails, ears, whiskers, eyes, body posture, and every hair on their bodies to communicate. Your child simply has to learn to listen with his eyes.

Here are some of the most common "words" or feelings a cat can express with just its tail. Once your child learns them, he'll literally be able to see the cat talk.

- Tail held straight in the air with no bends: a happy, enthusiastic "Hello."

21

- Held straight in the air but with a kink in the end: "Hello," but with reservations. There's something about the situation the cat dislikes.

- Tail curved gently down and then up again: "I'm at peace with the world."

- Raised slightly and softly curved: "I'm interested" or "I'm curious." His eyes may also be big and open, his ears perked up and swiveling, and his whiskers splayed wide and eagerly pointed ahead.

- Lowered fully and possibly tucked between the cat's hind legs: "I'm defeated." Mercy, mercy.

- Lowered and fluffed out: "I'm very afraid." His whiskers may also be flat against his face.

- Swishing violently from side to side: "I'm in conflict. I want to do something . . . yet then again, I don't want to do it."

- Held still but with tip twitching: "I'm mildly irritated."

- Held straight and fully bristled: "I'm getting mad."

- Arched and bristled or thrashing violently from side to side as the cat hisses: "I'm so angry, I'm about to attack."

As your child learns to read a cat's body language, he'll come to understand the cat better. But he'll also begin to notice that people send unspoken signals with their bodies, too. Over time, the peaceful, happy hours your child spends with the cat will make him more sensitive when communicating with people.

5. How to Hang a Spoon on Your Nose

A good time for laughing is when you can.
>—Jessamyn West, Cool Mom of much writing

Children have a silly-dilly nature. Giggles bubble up out of them as easily as crisp, cold spring water bubbles up out of the ground. At no time does a kid get to express this silly nature better than when she hangs a spoon on her nose. This feat of skill, ingenuity, and suspense has many entertaining uses. It can liven up a roadside lunch after a dull morning drive in the car, or just help her show off in the school lunchroom.

Hanging a spoon on one's nose requires only a metal teaspoon, a nose, and a little self-confidence. Here's the secret that makes the Cool Mom skill work: Your child needs to huff on the spoon to get it really fogged up. That's the only way it will stick.

First have your child shine up the spoon and her nose with a napkin. Now have her take a deep breath and gently exhale into the curved-in side of the spoon. Tell her to really fog it up. Then with her head held regally and tipped slightly back, she should gently but firmly press the spoon onto her nose. The tip of the spoon should be near the bridge of her nose. The part where the handle begins should be near the end of her nose. Have her press *firmly* on the back of the spoon for about five seconds. Once the spoon sticks, have her stop pressing and *slowly* remove her hand.

If the spoon flops into her lap, no problem. A few bungled tries only add to the suspense, making this feat look all the more difficult and all the more astounding when it's achieved. If the spoon falls, just have her once again fog it up and press it firmly against her nose. Eventually, the spoon will stay in place, dangling from her nose like a Christmas tree ornament.

She has just made a "spoon hang."

A spoon will hang on a nose for an amazingly long time. Some kids can do it for ten or fifteen minutes, even while walking up and down stairs.

Hanging a spoon on one's nose is the perfect antidote to boredom. At the same time, it upsets a kid's giggle box. With spoon-hanging thrown into the action, those family dinners just became even more fun. It's always good to have something new to add to the party.

6. How to Use a Yo-Yo

Fun doesn't always require a microchip.

—Cool Mom saying

The Greeks probably played with yo-yos twenty-five hundred years ago. Napoleon kept a yo-yo in his pocket. And the astronauts took yo-yos into outer space. So make your child part of this historic parade. Introduce him to the classically cool world of Yo. But do it right. Some kids can wow their friends with flashy tricks like "walk the dog," "skin the cat," and "rock the baby." Others can't even get their yo-yos to come back up the string.

The secret to doing lots of great tricks is this: Buy a yo-yo that will sleep a long time. Sleep? Yeah, that's when the yo-yo just spins at the end of its string. The yo-yo just hangs there, spinning, doing nothing. It's important that your kid's yo-yo be able to sleep well because nine in ten flashy yo-yo tricks involve throwing a wicked sleeper.

How do you know if a yo-yo will sleep a long time? It has to do with the type of yo-yo it is. A twist-apart yo-yo will usually sleep longer than the non-take-apart kind. If you want to go one cool step further, look for a new, improved yo-yo with a transaxle (a sleeve around the axle that cuts down on friction). Compared to the old-fashioned yo-yo, which was just glued together on a peg, transaxles sleep a lot longer. If the yo-yo also has a clutch, so much the better. With his first yo-yo, your child will need a little book of yo-yo tricks, too. Once you have a yo-yo that sleeps well, here's how to get your kid started.

First, your child should make sure the string is the right length. When the yo-yo touches the floor, the top of the string should come up to his belly button. If the string is longer than that, have him cut it off three inches above his belly button. He should then tie a one-inch loop on the end of the string. Now show him how to slip the string through this loop to create a second loop for his finger. He should slip the string on his middle finger between the first and second knuckles. Then have him wind the string around the axle until the yo-yo fits snugly into his palm against his middle finger.

To get ready to roll, have him hold the yo-yo in his palm up by his shoulder. His palm should be facing him, his elbow bent. Now have him cock his wrist and lower his forearm from shoulder height. With a flick of his wrist, the yo-yo will roll down the string. As it reaches the end of the string, but before it touches the ground, have him turn over his hand so his palm faces the ground. Give a quick lifting tug. The yo-yo should ride up the string and back into his palm.

If the yo-yo doesn't return, he may need to tighten the string by spinning the yo-yo in a clockwise direction. People who can't get their yo-yos to come back usually have the string too loose.

By teaching your kid how to use a yo-yo, you're giving

him a show-off skill he can carry around in his pocket. As he impresses his friends with his latest razzmatazz trick, he'll also learn that a toy requiring effort and skill can be a lot more fun than a toy that does everything for you. Self-confidence springs from doing stuff for yourself.

COOL MOM TIP

How to Make a Yo-Yo Sleep

When the yo-yo reaches the bottom of its string, your child should not give it the usual tug. Instead, he should just let it hang there, spinning on its axle. That's a sleeper. When it's time for the yo-yo to "wake up," have him give it a slight jerk, and it will ride up the string. If his yo-yo refuses to sleep, the string may be twisted too tight. To loosen the string, spin the yo-yo counterclockwise. How can he make his yo-yo sleep longer? Teach him the three keys to success: practice, practice, practice.

---

7. How to Avoid Strawberries

It would be a torture to get the clothes off. . . . I had strawberries on strawberries.

> —Sophie Kurys, who in 1946 set a
> world record for stolen bases

When playing baseball, sliding across hard-packed dirt into second base can be a bruising business. If a kid dives in head-first, she can jam her finger or hurt her face. If she goes in the correct way—feet first—she can wind up with strawberries.

Strawberries are small, purple red bruises a kid gets on her bottom and thighs when she slides into second base wrong. And, wow, do they hurt! They can even bleed. After the game, whenever she sits down, *ye-ouch!*

But you know a Cool Mom skill that will help your kid avoid strawberries. When going into second base feet first (the right way), she simply needs to hold her hands up in the air throughout the slide. That's all. When she raises her hands, she'll automatically lift her hip bones off the ground. And when she does—no strawberries.

When your kid is first learning to slide, have her do it the way they teach in baseball camps—barefoot on the grass. To make the grass slipperier and more slide-friendly, you may want to wet it down with a water hose.

With her right leg extended toward the base and her left

leg tucked under, so her legs resemble the number 4, she should aim for the base with her right foot as she slides. When she raises her hands in the air, she should be sliding into base on her left leg and hip pockets. Once she masters this move, have her practice using her left leg extended toward the base and her right leg tucked under.

Tell her that on any close play, she should slide straight into the bag—and slide *hard*. Being too timid or trying to dodge the tag will only cause her to slow down or get hurt.

Kids have a blast sliding around. And one day in that big game when your kid whooshes into second in a cloud of dust and the ump calls her safe, she'll also be safe from bruises. Which just goes to show that planning ahead is often the best way to save your butt.

COOL MOM FACTS

Legend of "The Flint Flash"

When Little Leaguers think about base-stealing heroes, they usually think of superstar Lou Brock, who stole 118 bases in a season, or Rickey Henderson, who stole 130. But another baseball legend beat both men by more than 70 steals. Who? Left fielder and second baseman Sophie Kurys, who played during World War II for the Racine Belles of the All-American Girls Baseball League. In 1946, Sophie (also known as "The Flint Flash") stole 201 bases out of 203 tries. And she did it bare-legged while wearing a skirt.

8. How to Talk in Code

Language alone is man's way of communicating with his fellow man, and it is language alone which separates him from the lower animals.
—Maya Angelou, Cool Mom of American poetry

In a world run on "adult talk," kids often feel like outsiders. But there is a way you can teach them "kid talk," so your child and his friends will always feel like insiders. Teach them to talk in code.

So what's the code? It's Pig Latin. If your child wants to say "Hello, Kathy," he says "Ellohay, athykay." If he wants to say "Billy is silly," he says "Illybay isyay illysay." Speaking Pig Latin is easy once you know the secret. And here it is: Your child simply has to change each word slightly, then add the sound -*ay* to the end.

Remind your child the vowels are A, E, I, O, U and sometimes Y. All the other letters are consonants. Once he remembers this, he only needs to follow three simple rules:

1. If a word starts with a vowel, simply add *yay* at the end. So Adam becomes Adamyay. Apple is appleyay. Awesome is awesomeyay.

2. If a word starts with one consonant, move the consonant to the end of the word and add -*ay*. So Sally becomes Allysay. Happy is appyhay. Silly is illysay. Yea! Yea! Yea! is Eayay! Eayay! Eayay!

3. If a word starts with a double consonant—like ch, sh, or th—move the entire double consonant sound to the end of the word and add *ay*. Child is ildchay. Think is inkthay.

Armed with these three rules, your kid will soon be rattling off whole paragraphs that sound like nonsense to an untutored ear, but make perfect sense to him. And when he asks "Ancay ouyay alktay igpay atinlay?"(Can you talk Pig Latin?), you'll instantly reply, "Ofyay oursecay! Ouldway ouyay ikelay omesay emonadelay?" (Of course! Would you like some lemonade?)

Speaking Pig Latin involves exercising grammar skills, which may be why kids who learn this secret code often become better readers. This skill also requires that your child think before he speaks. How else are you going to get a kid to do that?

COOL MOM TIP

Talking Pig Latin on the Internet

Once your child masters Pig Latin, show him how popular "his" language has become. Get on the Internet and take him to the Igpay Atinlay Google search engine at *www.google.com/intl/xx-piglatin/*. That's right. There' a whole Internet search engine devoted to Pig Latin! E'llhay ovelay ityay. (He'll love it.)

9. How to Identify a Poisonous Spider

Those who dwell, as scientists or laymen, among the beauties
and mysteries of the earth are never alone or weary of life.
　　　　　　　　　　　　—Rachel Carson, Cool Mom of the
　　　　　　　　　　　　modern environmental movement

With those eight crawly legs wiggling in all directions, spiders resemble tiny, land-based octopuses. Then one day a kid hears that some spiders have poisonous bites. The magic just went out of spiders. Wonder is replaced by fear. Suddenly, every time the child sees a spider, she wants to kill it.

With a little insight, you can give your child relief from empty-headed fears. Teach her how to tell immediately if a spider is poisonous. Of the fifty thousand types of spiders in the world, only four in the U.S. are poisonous. With spiders, *poisonous* doesn't always mean fatal. It just means the bite can make you sick. Fortunately, all four carry one or more clear warning signs (noted in italics below).

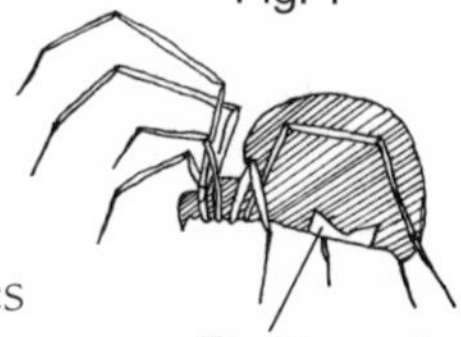

The Black Widow (Fig. 1): This half-inch-long spider has a shiny black body and *a red "hourglass" on its tummy*. It lives in dark places like closets, attics, and piles

Fig. 1

Red hourglass

of firewood. Anyone bitten by this spider should see a doctor, but shouldn't panic. No one in the U.S. has died from a black widow spider bite in years.

The Brown Recluse (Fig. 2): About half an inch long, this light brown spider often has *a dark violin mark* that starts at the spider's eyes and points toward its "waist." It also has *six eyes* (most spiders have eight) and *no markings on its tail* segment. This secretive spider hides in dark, out-of-the-way places and is found only in the South and Midwest.

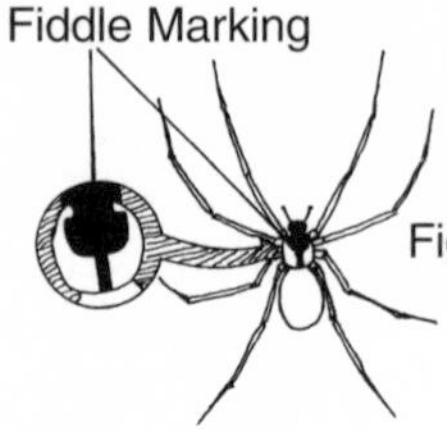

Fiddle Marking

Fig. 2

The Hobo Spider (Fig. 3): This small, brown spider builds small, funnel-shaped webs close to the ground, then lies in wait for his prey. Between his two front legs he carries *two large palps that resemble boxing gloves*. On top of his abdomen are *dark chevrons*, which fade with age. He lives mostly in Washington, Idaho, Oregon, and parts of Utah.

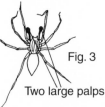

Fig. 3

Two large palps

The Yellow Sac Spider (Fig. 4): This small spider (the male's about one-quarter inch long) is *all yellow*. It makes its home under foliage when it can,

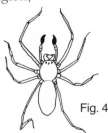

Fig. 4

but if it can't, it prefers houses. The yellow sac spider has a wide range. It has been spotted in Eastern cities as well as the West and Northwest.

Most spiders inject poison only while hunting for food. If they bite in self-defense, they don't inject poison, but infection can set in. If your child is ever bitten by one of these spiders, go to a doctor immediately, but don't panic.

Like most prejudices, the fear of spiders will vanish as your child gains a greater understanding of nature's mysteries. Curiosity leads to exploring. And exploring produces new knowledge that destroys mindless fears.

10. How to Write a Thank-You Note

Etiquette—a fancy word for simple kindness.
—Elsa Maxwell, Cool Mom of many great parties

When it's time to write a thank-you note, most kids have no idea how to fill that blank sheet of paper. So they dilly-dally around, delaying the task until six months have passed. By then, it's so late *any* note sounds ungrateful.

Fortunately, you know a secret that will help your child write a thank-you note deftly and promptly. The secret is this: Have him tell a brief story about the gift or occasion. He should focus on how good the gift or occasion made him feel or how it has improved his life in some small but meaningful way.

For example, instead of writing, "Thanks for the trip to Disney World. I really liked it," your son might say, "I loved Peter Pan's Flight best. I can still hear Peter say as we sail out the window, 'And awaaaay, we go!'" Or in place of a terse "Thanks for the sweater. It's my favorite color," your daughter might send Aunt Em a note saying, "I wore your beautifully knit sweater to school yesterday, and everyone commented on how perfectly the blue in the sweater matched the color of my eyes."

What if it's an inappropriate or dreadful gift—a pair of

ugly brown socks when your kid was dying for a video game? Then a bit more tact is required. Although he mustn't hurt the person's feelings, your child needn't lie. As Emily Post, the Cool Mom of manners, cleverly puts it: "It is quite possible to find a phrase that can be taken to mean anything the recipient wishes." Some examples:

> "The George Burns and Gracie Allen action figures are fascinating—my friends can't stop talking about them."

> "The Elmer Fudd night light is unique. I've never before seen anything like it."

> "Thank you for the brown socks. They're really warm, and they go great with my brown shoes."

None of these comments is untrue, and they suggest your child enjoyed the gift, although they don't actually say so.

By teaching your child to write a gracious thank-you note, you're teaching him how important it is to respect others' rights and consider their feelings. In the end, good manners are merely a matter of applying the Golden Rule: Do unto others as you would have them do unto you.

11. How to Throw a Spiral Pass

The best-educated human being is the one who understands most about the life in which he is placed.
—Helen Keller, Cool Mom of an inspiring and heroic life

Your kid is a sensational passer—in her dreams. She can imagine herself uncorking a long bomb that's caught in the end zone. She wins the game! But when she gets on the field for real, the dream bubble bursts. Her passes wobble, float, and fly like big dodo birds. Then they die ten feet short of her receivers. She's muddled. What's she doing wrong?

Well, the problem is plain. The kid doesn't know how to throw a spiral pass. A spiral pass will turn those wounded dodos into rockets that streak down field, then land like docile little doves in the receiver's arms. Teaching a kid how to throw a crisp spiral is surprisingly easy. You just need to teach her the secret of the overhand grip.

First, have your kid place her hand well back on the football, spreading her fingers as wide as she can. She should grip with only her fingertips. The ball should never touch the heel of her palm. Only her pinkie and ring finger tips should touch the laces. Her middle and index fingers should be over the seam that runs from the laces to the back point of the ball (Fig. 1). Have her stretch her index finger back as far as she can until it's almost at the back point of the ball. Her index finger will direct the ball as it's released. As she throws the ball, it will roll off her fingertips from little finger to index finger. This rolling motion makes the ball spiral.

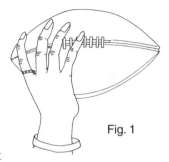

Fig. 1

Some pros use a second grip called the thumb grip (the thumb is on the laces or above it). But tell your kid not to worry about that. To use it, the passer needs big hands and long fingers. For a child, the overhand grip is much better.

A kid who knows how to throw a spiral with four tacklers coming at her learns a lot about maintaining her poise in a clutch. At the same time, she's learning it's great to have dreams. But to achieve those dreams, she often needs to rely on sound forms worked out by others.

COOL MOM TIP

Buying the Right Size Football

Footballs come in many sizes. Your child should start with a small one. A regular-sized football is too big for a child's hands. If it's too big, she can't hold it right and can't throw a spiral. How do you know if a ball's too big? Have your kid place her palm over the middle of the ball. If she can pick up the ball with one hand and toss it in the air, it's the right size.

12. How to Win a Video Game

Calm your mind. . . . No problem can be solved by a drunken monkey.

—Emily Arnold McCully, Cool Mom of the children's book *Beautiful Warrior*

*B*onka, bonka, blip, poink, pink, dakka, dakka, dakka. You peek around the corner into the living room. Just as you thought. Your kid's at it again. He's playing his two hundredth video game for the week. Well, maybe not the two hundredth. Maybe only the tenth or twelfth. But you're sure he's addicted. What's worse, he's not having fun. Each time he loses, he gets angry and throws a fit of frustration. Three minutes later, he's back at it again, his glazed eyes locked on the screen. *Bonka, bonka, blip, poink, pink, dakka, dakka, dakka.* And still he keeps losing.

Fortunately, you don't have to teach your kid how to stop being a sore loser. You know how he can play video games and *win.* The secret: Tell him to keep his cool and stop blaming himself.

The great advantage of a video game over life is that a video game keeps repeating itself. If your kid makes a mistake, he can have a second chance . . . and a third . . . and a fourth. By keeping his head, he'll be able to figure out where he went wrong, and he won't keep repeating the same mistake.

Many kids who play video games want so desperately to win they can't think straight when they lose. They forget they're playing this game to have *fun*. So if your kid keeps losing, tell him to avoid diving immediately back into the game. Instead, pause, take a deep breath, go read a book—maybe put away the game until tomorrow. Our brains do miraculous work for us as we sleep: They solve problems. When he starts fresh the next day, your child may find the problem in the game that previously had him stuck for four hours can now be solved in ten minutes.

If he kicks back, relaxes, but still has no fun, it's probably not his fault. The game may be too hard for him at his age. (Most games have difficulty levels. Make sure his game is set on "easy.") If he still has trouble, play the game with him. You may find the game's so poorly designed, it's no fun for anyone. In this case, life's too short to play bad video games. Get him another game that plays better.

The child who learns how to play a video game—and *win*—learns a lot about patiently hanging in and not blaming himself when the going gets tough. He learns how to play hard without getting mad. *Boink, boink, pink, plink, KABLOOEY, KABLOOEY, KABLOOEY!* Sometimes we just have to relax and let the good times roll.

13. How to Make Peanut Butter from Scratch

Peanut butter is the pâté of childhood.
    —Florence Fabricant, Cool Mom of many food columns

According to the National Peanut Board, the average child will eat fifteen hundred peanut-butter-and-jelly sandwiches before graduating from high school. Most kids would much rather eat peanut butter than eat their beans. But what is that yummy golden-brown paste between those two slices of bread? Sure, most kids know it's made out of peanuts—somehow. But that's where their knowledge starts and stops. So demystify a part of childhood. Show your kid how to make peanut butter from scratch. What's really neat about this: If she likes the crunchy kind, she can add lots of extra crunch. She can make peanuttier butter.

You don't mind if she makes a big batch. That's because you know a secret your child doesn't know. Peanuts are not actually nuts. They're *peas*. So by eating the peanut butter she makes herself (surprise! surprise!), your kid is eating quite healthy.

To make peanut butter from all-natural ingredients, one needs only some peanuts, butter or peanut oil, a blender, and a food processor (if she wants crunchy).

Here's a recipe for one cup of peanut butter that's so simple any kid can follow it:

2 cups of shelled peanuts
2 teaspoons butter or peanut oil
⅛ teaspoon salt, or more (whatever tastes best to her)

Put the nuts in a pan of boiling water for one minute. Then remove the skins. Now put half the nuts in a blender on high for one minute. Use a spatula to scrape the nuts down the sides of the blender. Spin the nuts in the blender for another minute. Add the butter or peanut oil and the salt. Repeat this process with the second cup of nuts.

To make the crunchy type, save back one-third of the nuts and coarsely grind them in a food processor. Then have your child mix them in with the peanut butter she made in the blender. If she wants more crunch, she can save back more peanuts.

The joy of making peanut butter from scratch is that your child can adjust the ingredients to get the texture and flavor she likes best. And when she's done, she can make a peanut-tier-butter sandwich. Now she'll just have one more question: Got milk?

COOL MOM FACTS

- The world's largest peanut-butter-and-jelly sandwich was 40 feet long and was created in Peanut, Pennsylvania. It contained 150 pounds of peanut butter and 50 pounds of jelly.

- One acre of peanuts will make about 30,000 peanut-butter sandwiches.

14. How to Use Pliers

You're only as competent as your tools. So you'd better learn how to use them.

—Cool Mom saying

The bright kid who plays with toy tools quickly grows bored. Why? Because toy tools are klutzy. The plastic saw won't cut wood. The toy hammer won't drive nails. Trying to learn how to use a real tool by playing with a toy is like trying to learn how to ride a real pony by playing with a rocking horse.

So teach your child how to use real tools that do real jobs. One good starter tool for most kids is a pair of pliers. Pliers come in many different types: duck bill, side-cutting, long-nosed. But the most common type—and a good one for any kid to learn to use as soon as he's ready—is the slip-joint combination pliers.

Your child can use this versatile tool to do anything from attaching a reflector to the back of his bike to wiring a water bottle into his guinea pig cage. The possibilities are limited only by his needs of the moment and his own ingenuity.

When you give your child his first pair of pliers, point out the grooved jaws and the bolt (also known as a pivot pin), with which the jaws are fastened together (Fig. 1). Show him

how he can use the
pivot pin to move the
jaws to either of two
positions: wide (which
will help him grasp
large objects) and not-
so-wide (for smaller
objects).

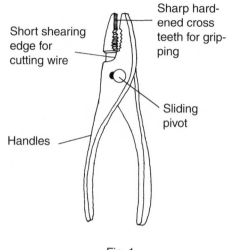

Short shearing
edge for
cutting wire

Sharp hard-
ened cross
teeth for grip-
ping

Sliding
pivot

Handles

Fig. 1

To open the jaws,
he should spread the
ends of the handles as
far apart as possible.
The slip-joint, or pivot,
can now be moved to a
wider setting for larger
objects. To bring the
jaws closer together for smaller objects, he should again
spread the handles as far as possible, then push the joint back
into the original position.

Now have him use the pliers to perform some simple
task. If the cat has batted its catnip mouse out of reach
under the sofa, for example, he can use his pliers to retrieve
it. Give him a few small wires and let him wire stuff together
for a while.

By learning to use slip-joint pliers, your child has just
stretched his ability to deal with the world. He has added an
elegant solution to his repertoire that's been around for perhaps thousands of years. And that's what real tools always do:

They give us elegant solutions to help solve our problems. Your kid will outgrow many things every year. Using a tool won't be one of them.

COOL MOM TIP

Tell your child he should never use pliers to turn a metal nut. That's because a pair of pliers can damage a nut in just a few seconds. Pliers must never be substituted for wrenches (see 73, How to Use a Wrench). Also, before he stores his pliers in a toolbox, have him coat the tool with a few drops of light oil, to keep it from rusting.

15. How to Spin a Basketball on One Finger

No matter how many times you drop the ball, keep trying. Great success is often built on many tiny defeats.

—Cool Mom saying

Little kids are easy to impress. You can read, and they can't. Cool! You can write in *longhand*. Cool! You can snap your fingers, bake gingerbread men, and cross your eyes. Triple cool! As kids grow older, you're no less cool. But they grow more jaded. Your kid may even dare to imagine she knows more than you do (not!). That's when it's time to up the ante and bring in the big guns. It's time to teach her how to spin a basketball on one finger.

This skill is especially dazzling because only a few people (mostly NBA superstars) can do it. Your kid needs to place and keep her finger exactly in dead center under the ball. But how does she find dead center? She could spend a month of practice trying to find it, but there is an easier way: Put the ball in a large bowl of water and use a felt-tipped pen to mark the spot that ends up on the bottom. Make a spot about the size of a nickel. That's the heavy point of the ball—the South Pole—the place where her finger needs to stay to keep the ball spinning.

Start with a slightly under-inflated ball, which is much easier to balance. Have your child hold the ball with her fingertips. Assuming she's right-handed, have her place her left hand on top, her right hand under the ball. Her right palm should be directly under the dead-center spot.

With a quick flick of her right wrist, have her send the ball spinning clockwise or counterclockwise (whichever feels most comfortable to her). As the ball spins, it will automatically rise in the air—just long enough for her to slip her finger quickly under the ball right on the dead-center spot. Now have her remove her top hand from the ball.

Most people spin a basketball on their index finger. But some use a middle or ring finger. A few NBA stars even use a fingernail. As the ball spins, tell your kid to keep her finger perfectly straight, pointed directly up toward the sky.

At first, of course, when she lets go of the ball, it will career across the room or the yard. But with patience and perseverance, she'll get it. And when she does, she'll realize you still have a few tricks up your sleeve. Watch out, kids; Mom's on the move. She never quits, and you shouldn't either.

16. How to Hike Yourself Rested

I can remember walking as a child. It was not customary to say you were fatigued. It was customary to complete the goal of the expedition.

—Katherine Hepburn, Cool Mom of *The African Queen*

Whether you're sightseeing on vacation or hiking in the wild, there comes a time in every family's day when it's getting late and the end of your walk is nowhere in sight. The kids are starting to groan about their aching legs. Promising "we'll be there shortly" does not stop the complaining.

But you know a Cool Mom skill that will relieve those tired legs and do away with the whining. You know how your kids can rest *while* they walk. The secret is an old mountaineer's trick called the "rest step." When a kid walks a long distance, pain mounts as lactic acid builds up in the muscles around his knee. The rest step takes pressure off his knees just for a split second. But it's long enough to wash away the lactic acid. As a result, the pain surprisingly disappears.

Here's how it works: As your child steps forward, tell him to let his leg go limp for a second before he puts his weight on it. Or, if he'd rather, he can let his back leg go limp. It's the limping that's important. As he limps up the hill, he may look a bit like a drunken sailor. But the sillier he feels, the more fun he'll have. Soon his second wind will kick in, and you may find it hard to keep up with him.

The kids will arrive at your destination almost refreshed. You won't be irritable from listening to all that moaning. At the same time, your children will have learned a little lesson about finishing what you start. It doesn't matter how long it takes to get there. What counts is that you keep moving forward.

COOL MOM TIP

The Robot Rest Step

It's often good to have a second secret in your knapsack. So here's another rest step often taught in mountaineering schools. As your child steps forward with his right foot, have him straighten his right leg and lock his knee. As he shifts his weight onto his right leg, have him lift and deeply flex his left leg to rest it and get the blood circulating through it. Now have him straighten and lock his left knee, put his weight on his left leg, and deeply flex and lift his right leg. He'll look a bit like a robot walking uphill, but he'll soon feel better. If you have two or three kids, they may even strike up a contest to see who can do the silliest walk.

17. How to Multiply by Nine on Your Fingers

I see a certain order to the universe and math is one way of making it visible.

—U.S. poet and author May Sarton

Some kids do just fine in math—until the monstrous multiplication tables rear their ugly heads. Suddenly, math fear erupts. The higher the number, the more some kids become anxious. They get that glazed, terrified look in their eyes whenever they have to multiply any number by nine. They fall behind. And later in life, they may find their opportunities limited because they're math illiterate.

But your child acquires a certain confidence around math. That's because you know a Cool Mom skill that will jog her memory whenever she has to multiply by nine. It's as simple as counting on her fingers.

First, have your child lay her hands palm-down on a desk or table, extending her fingers. Assign each finger a number—one through ten, from left to right (Fig. 1). Now show her the secret. To find nine times seven, have her lift the number seven finger. Now have her observe the amazing fact: There are six fingers to its left and three to its right. Six and three is sixty-three. And nine times seven equals sixty-three.

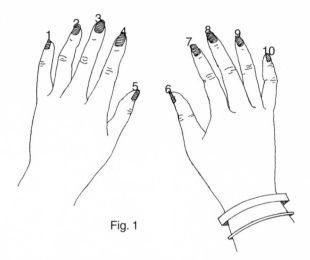

Fig. 1

Her fingers got the right answer! Let's try it again with nine times five. Have her lift the number five finger (which happens to be her left thumb). The four fingers to the left of her thumb and the five on her right hand make four and five or forty-five. And, yes indeed, nine times five does equal forty-five. It's truly amazing. This secret works all the way up to nine times ten.

As your kid learns this shortcut way of multiplying by nine, she's also learning that numbers have some wondrous properties. Once she gets curious about these properties, she may go on to become quite fond of mathematics. But even if she doesn't, she'll still have learned that math should never be feared. It's just another handy method she can use to become more effective in the world.

18. How to Make a Paper Cup

Never let anyone convince you that you don't have what it takes to accomplish your dreams. With a little ingenuity, an ordinary piece of paper can become an extraordinary cup.

—Cool Mom saying

The cup is one of the great assets of civilization. With a cup, a human can dip water from a spring, lift it to his lips, and drink while standing erect. No one knows how long it took people to develop the cup. But it must have been thousands of years. With a simple, flat sheet of paper, your amazed child can travel across those thousands of years and recreate the cup for himself.

This cup is folded in such a clever way that every spot where the liquid would normally run *down* and *out* is folded *up* and *in*. As a result, gravity keeps the paper liquid-tight. Your kid won't lose any of his drink.

Have your child start with a square piece of white paper— no lines, no writing (any ink on the paper could leak into the drink). Now it's as easy as one, two, three, four.

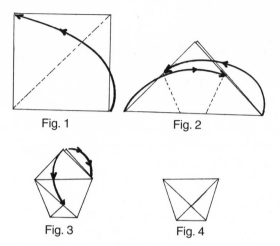

Fig. 1   Fig. 2

Fig. 3   Fig. 4

1. Fold the square in half to form a triangle (Fig. 1).
2. Fold over the two lower corners of the triangle as shown (Fig. 2).
3. Fold the two upper triangles down on each side of the cup (Fig. 3).
4. And *voila!* the cup (Fig. 4). Open the top.

With just a flat piece of paper, your competent child has created a cup he can now fill with his favorite drink.

At the same time, he may just have gained more appreciation for man's ingenuity. Paper that touches water usually becomes drenched and falls apart. But with a little practical know-how, your child can make paper hold water. There's something very satisfying about a well-crafted cup.

19. How to See Better in the Dark

You gain strength, courage, and confidence by every experience in which you really stop to look fear in the face. You must do the thing which you think you cannot do.

—Eleanor Roosevelt, Cool Mom of the White House

The night is a friendly time, filled with chirping crickets, flickering fireflies, and moonbeams. In the gentle darkness, a child can see to the ends of the universe and be on intimate terms with the most distant stars. Yet many children find the dark terrifying. It's not what your child can see in the dark she finds scary. It's what she *can't* see that freaks her out.

So teach your child how to see better in the dark. Here's the secret: She has to look slightly off to one side of any object she's observing. To see better in the dark, she needs to use what astronomers call "averted vision."

Explain to your child that when she looks directly at any object, she's using the center part of her eye, or iris. This part of her eye is packed with cone cells (which see best in bright, strong light). When she looks slightly to one side of an object, the light strikes that off-the-center part of her eye that has more rod cells (which see better in the dark).

To teach your child how to use averted vision, take her outside on a clear night. Have her pick out a star that looks dim. Tell her to notice that when she stares at the star directly, it grows dimmer. It may even disappear. Why? Because her cones (in the centers of her eyes) don't work well in the dark. Now have her avert her gaze slightly and look just to one side of the star. With a little adjustment of her eyes, she'll discover the star looks brighter than when she was staring at it straight on! Learning averted vision takes patience and practice. So have your child fiddle with it a bit, first looking at the star directly, then sideways. Eventually, she'll detect a difference.

After your child has had fun exploring the stars with averted vision, take her into her room and sit beside her on the bed. Have her look at several familiar objects. How does the dark change how everything in her room looks? Have her use her new "night vision" to look at her dresser and that large teddy bear in the corner. She'll find that the longer she looks at an object using averted vision (up to six seconds), the more detail she'll pick up.

Many adults equate darkness with evil. Children pick up on this association and get scared. By learning to see better in the dark, your kid will come to understand that goodness fills the universe like moonlight fills the night, only without shadow. And the once-scary dark will just have gotten more friendly.

COOL MOM FACT

Most animals who hunt at night, such as raccoons, cats, and skunks, have a lot more rods in their eyes than people do. That's why they can see a lot better at night than we can. But they also have no cones in their eyes. That's why they can't see color.

20. How to Make the World's Best Caramel Corn

A good cook is like a sorceress who dispenses happiness.
—Elsa Schiaparelli, Cool Mom of high fashion

All kids love homemade food. And what better food to fill a cool afternoon than homemade caramel corn? Whether it's for Halloween, Christmas, or just to lift everyone's spirits on a rainy day, there's magic in a well-planned recipe.

When a kid sees a box of sugar, he sees only sugar. Salt is just salt. Butter is just butter. But you know that when all those ingredients are mixed together, a new up-until-now-never-heard-of-before flavor emerges. And . . . well, that's cooking. Learning this skill will delight your child and teach him how to cook at the same time.

As a Cool Mom knows, the secret to any delectable cuisine lies in the recipe. And here's the very best recipe for caramel corn ever devised:

2 bags light microwave popcorn
1 cup butter
1 box light brown sugar
½ cup light corn syrup
½ teaspoon salt

1 teaspoon vanilla
½ teaspoon baking soda

Have your child pop each bag of popcorn (one at a time) in the microwave, as directed on the package, being careful as he removes the hot bags from the oven. Now have him pour the popcorn into a large baking pan. Preheat the oven to 250 degrees. As the oven heats, combine the butter, brown sugar, corn syrup, and salt into a two-quart saucepan. Heat to a roiling boil. Turn down the heat to medium and let the contents of the pan continue to boil for five minutes without stirring. Remove from the heat. Add the vanilla and baking soda and stir. The baking soda will cause the syrup to almost double in bulk.

Have your child pour the syrup over the popcorn, stirring to coat as much of the popcorn as possible. Now have him bake the popcorn for one hour in the oven, stirring it every fifteen minutes with a spatula or plastic pancake turner to keep it well-coated with caramel. At the end of the hour, remove the pan from the oven and spread the popcorn onto ungreased aluminum foil. Once the caramel corn cools, your child can break up any large chunks into smaller pieces.

The kid who can make his own caramel corn will come to understand that good cooking has magic in it. The magic comes from all those ingredients. One ingredient makes for a dull dish. But thoroughly mixing many flavors together in the right proportions and under the right conditions creates a truly spell-binding treat. As he crunches happily away, he may also recall another old saying: Nothin' says lovin' like somethin' from the oven.

21. How to Trap a Spider Web

Look on everything as though you were seeing it either for the first or last time. Then your time on earth will be filled with glory.
—Betty Smith, Cool Mom of *A Tree Grows in Brooklyn*

Getting a close-up look at a spider web is like trying to trap a sunbeam. A spider web can stretch from branch to branch on a rosebush like a mighty fortress. But let a child try to touch one, and it breaks away and vanishes in grey wisps on the wind—unless you know the secret that will let her observe a spider web in all its fragile wonder.

The secret is this: talcum powder. Have your child gently blow a shower of very fine talcum powder over the web. Now she can see all its intricate detail.

To trap or "capture" the web, have your child lightly spray some glue (the kind available at an art supply or craft store) onto a black piece of cardboard. (If you have no glue, try hair spray.) Then have her move the cardboard toward the web very gently. She should move slowly and patiently, until all parts of the web touch the cardboard at once. This way, the web will stick to the cardboard without being damaged. As soon as the web touches the cardboard, have her take tiny nail scissors and gently cut the support threads away from the branches. The web can now be lifted from the rosebush and carried away. When trying this for the first time, try to locate several webs before you begin. That way if one web falls apart, she can go immediately on to another.

Capturing a treasure as fragile as a spider web requires exercising patience and ingenuity. And as your child admires the web with wide-eyed enchantment, she'll feel closer to her own deeper truths. When we allow nature to be torn apart and polluted, it offers no insights or solace. But when it's intact and innocent, we discover ourselves.

COOL MOM FACTS

- Spiders have been spinning their webs for 300 million years—before dinosaurs walked the earth.

- Spiders catch tons of insects. If you were to add up the weight of all the insects spiders eat in a year, it would total more than the weight of all the people on Earth.

- Spider silk is incredibly strong. It's said that a single strand of spider silk, if it were as thick as a pencil, could stop a 747 in flight.

- Spider blood is pale blue.

- Most spiders don't jump at people. But there is one—the jumping spider—that can leap up to twenty-five times its own body length. That would be like a three-year-old jumping as high as a seven-story building. No wonder Stan Lee (who created characters for Marvel comics) named one of his superheroes Spider-Man!

22. How to Tell How Far North You Are

Self-trust, we know, is the first secret of success.
—Lady Jane Wilde, Cool Mom of English poetry

When kids get curious about their place on this planet, they think all the answers lie in globes and atlases. Unfortunately, they may find those dull. But you know a globe or atlas is only a map of God's reality. So after your child has learned about the equator in school, ask, "Would you like to figure out for yourself how far north of the equator we live?"

When he looks mystified, tell him it's easy. He needs only an object he can see on any clear night (the North Star) and a tool he always has with him (his hand).

The secret about the North Star (Polaris) is that once he finds it from a specific point on the Earth, it never moves. It's always in the same spot in the sky. At the equator, Polaris is always on the horizon. At the North Pole, it's always directly overhead. In the United States (except for Hawaii and Alaska), Polaris is always about halfway up the sky.

So take your child outside on any starry night to a spot with a clear view of the sky, and help him find Polaris. First, look for the Big Dipper. It's one of the most obvious star patterns in the sky. Once you've found it, point out the two stars at the outer edge of the Big Dipper's cup. One is Merak. The other is Dubhe. These are the "pointer stars." They point to Polaris (Fig. 1).

Now have your child use his hand as a measuring device to tell how many degrees Polaris is up from the horizon. When he holds his hand out at arm's length from his eyes (Fig. 2), his hand covers 10 degrees in the sky. One finger covers 2 degrees. His hand spread wide (Fig. 3) covers 20 degrees.

Have him use his hand to count the number of degrees from the horizon up to Polaris. He'll probably get a number between twenty-five and forty-nine. That's the number of

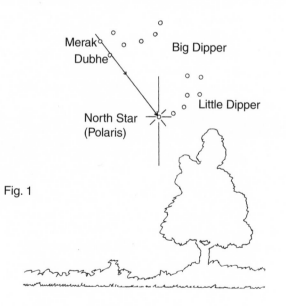

Fig. 1

degrees north he is from the equator. To change those degrees into miles, have him multiply by sixty-nine (the number of miles in a degree).

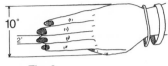

Fig. 2

Let's say he finds Polaris 37 degrees above the horizon. Then thirty-seven times sixty-nine equals the number of miles north of the equator he is. About 2,550 miles. Tell him he has just used a secret that travelers have used for thousands of years to keep from getting lost.

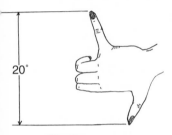

Fig. 3

As your child ponders all this, it may dawn on him that he doesn't always have to depend on others to tell him where he stands. He can figure it out for himself.

COOL MOM FACT

How can your hand and your child's much smaller hand both measure the same number of degrees in the sky? It's the way angles work. Your child's hand is *smaller,* but his arm is also shorter than yours. As a result, the angle in the sky he measures with his hand will be almost exactly the same as the angle you measure with yours.

23. How to Fix a Bicycle Chain

A child who can fix a broken bicycle chain is as capable as an adult who can repair a car engine.

—Cool Mom observation

Give a child a bicycle, and you've made her self-reliant. She can travel many places without begging rides. Teach her how to repair a bicycle chain, and you've made her independent. When her bike breaks down, she can get it going again.

Of course, you know the secret to fixing a bent or broken link in a bicycle chain: Use a chain tool, also called a rivet extractor (Fig. 1). With a chain tool, which costs only a few bucks at any bicycle store, she can fix that link on her own. Make sure she gets the right chain tool. Some chains (such as one called a Hyper-Glide chain) require their own special tool.

Before she begins, have her

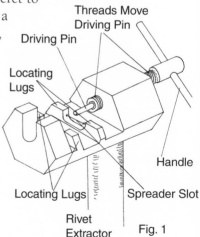

Threads Move Driving Pin

Driving Pin

Locating Lugs

Handle

Locating Lugs

Spreader Slot

Rivet Extractor

Fig. 1

inspect the chain (Fig.2) to see how it
works. Have her notice each link
has an inner plate and an outer
plate. Once she sees how the
chain works, have her practice
on an old section of chain and
follow these steps:

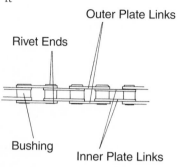

Fig. 2

1. Place the chain in the tool
(Fig. 3) so the rivet that needs to
be pushed out is in the slot
between the two locating lugs farthest from the handle. Tighten the
driving pin to hold the link firmly in
place. She should make sure the driving pin is *exactly* aligned
with the rivet she wants to remove.

2. Slowly keep rotating the chain tool handle (about 6
turns) until the rivet clears both inner link plates but is still
held in place by the outer link plate farthest from the handle.

3. Take the chain out of the tool, and flex the chain to
remove the link. Don't let the rivet pop out of the outer link
plate. Rivets are tough to replace if they're taken out.

4. Position the chain in the tool between the locating lugs
closest to the handle. Make sure the rivet to be driven back in
lines up exactly with the driving pin.

5. With the new rivet against the driving pin, tighten the
handle to drive the rivet in. If it sticks, back off and wiggle
the link to line the rivet up with the hole and try again. Never
use excess force.

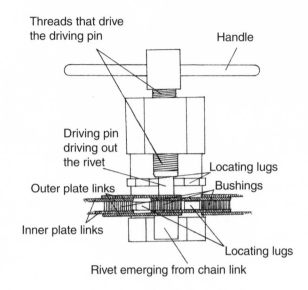

Threads that drive the driving pin

Handle

Driving pin driving out the rivet

Locating lugs

Outer plate links

Bushings

Inner plate links

Locating lugs

Rivet emerging from chain link

Fig. 3

6. Stop driving in the rivet when the end of it just peeks through the outer plate farthest from the handle.

7. Gently, with half a turn or so, tighten the handle until both ends of the rivet stick just slightly out of both outer link plates.

Learning to repair her own bicycle chain will build your child's confidence and inspire independence. Much as we might like for them to, people can't go around fixing all our problems. Even when we're part of a loving family and community, we must always remember others are counting on us to solve our own problems and give them time to solve theirs.

24. How to Wrap a Gift

It is not how much we do, but how much love we put into the doing.
—Mother Teresa, Cool "Mom" of the Calcutta sick and poor

At Christmas or on birthdays, the shimmering wrapping papers and shiny satin bows make a joy of the presents. The care with which a box was wrapped reflects how much love went into the gift. But let a kid try to wrap a present for someone else, and gloom sets in. Soon the paper's wadded in a crunched mess, yards of ribbon lie tangled on the floor, and the kid's got his fingers taped to the box.

Happily, you know how to free your open-hearted kid from such a dark disaster. The trick to wrapping a gift lies in neatly trimming the paper to the correct size. To do that, your child can follow these steps:

1. Measure the amount of the paper needed by wrapping it lengthwise around the box (Fig. 1). Use scissors to trim the paper to the size needed.

2. Check to see how much paper will be required to cover the ends of the box (Fig. 1). Make sure he does this step correctly. If he trims off too much paper, it won't cover the ends. If he trims off too little, he'll just have wads of paper at the end of the box.

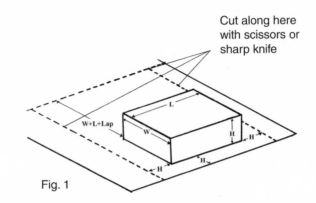

Cut along here
with scissors or
sharp knife

L

W+L+Lap

W

H

H

H

H

Fig. 1

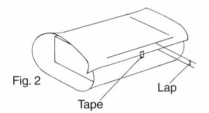

Fig. 2

Lap

Tape

Fig. 3

Fold in flat against ends

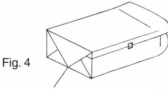

Fig. 4

If point goes beyond edge,
fold down

3. Fold the paper around the box, taping it to one side (Fig. 2).

4. Fold the paper on one end of the box, as shown (Fig.3).

5. Fold the triangle of paper up and tape it to the end of the box. Then fold the other triangle of paper down and tape it to the box (Fig.4).

6. Repeat steps 4 and 5 on the other end of the box.

Once your kid has a crisply wrapped box, he can add a flashy store-bought ribbon. He'll soon have a gift as dazzling as any Santa will deliver. By taking care to wrap the present elegantly, he'll discover a task that looks hard often becomes easy when you divide it into a series of small steps. Behind all beauty lies a plan, even if we can't always see it.

25. How to Cruise on a Skateboard

You're a girl, so you can do it, if you just keep trying.
　　—Lyn-Z Adams, Cool Mom of competitive skateboarding

Of all toys, the skateboard is arguably the coolest. No one looks more self-possessed than the kid cruising down the street on her "surfboard on wheels," the breeze ruffling her hair. And no one looks dorkier than the kid who keeps falling off.

So teach your kid how to ride her skateboard with style. The secret to learning to cruise smoothly on a skateboard is to grasp the fundamentals a little at a time. Start slow and work up.

For safety's sake, your child should wear a helmet, knee and elbow pads, gloves, and long sleeves. Have her practice only on a smooth, debris-free sidewalk or parking lot—somewhere free of vehicles and pedestrians. Start by having her step up on the board with the foot with which she feels most comfortable. Let's say she chooses to put her left foot on the board. Now have her kick the ground with her right foot to propel the board forward.

Once she's comfortable with this move and can zip along at a reasonable pace, it's time to cruise. Have her put her right foot up on the board behind her left foot at a 45-degree angle. Then have her adjust her left foot until it's parallel with the right one.

When she's in the correct position, she'll be standing on the board half sideways. For balance, have her bend her knees slightly and lean forward. To turn, she should lean slightly in the direction she wants to go. Have her lean with her hips (not from her waist). When she wants to get off the board, she simply jumps off in the direction she's facing. To keep from losing her balance, she needs to land on the ground at a run.

Once she can cruise on the level, it's time to coast down a hill. Remember, she has to learn everything gradually. Find a gently sloping hill that looks safe (no nearby traffic or walls to run into). Have her mount the board and bend her knees slightly. Make sure she looks ahead and doesn't just stare at her feet. For balance, she should keep her arms forward in front of her body and her weight centered on the board. If she starts coasting too fast, she can slow down by leaning slightly from side to side with her hips and running down the hill in a zig-zag pattern, much as a skier slaloms down a mountain slope.

Skateboarding offers a thrill a minute and a valuable education. As your child slowly gains poise and confidence, she's also learning the knack of keeping her mental balance while moving fast. In this fast-paced world, that's a handy skill for anybody to know.

COOL MOM FACT

It was in 1977 that skateboarding became a national sport. That was the year the first article about skateboarding appeared in the pages of *Sports Illustrated.*

26. How to Get a Close-Up Look at a Hummingbird

Those who contemplate the beauty of the earth find reserves of strength that will endure as long as life lasts.

—Rachel Carson, Cool Mom of the
modern environmental movement

Hummingbirds look so colorful and exotic, it's as if they had arrived on a magic carpet from India, or better yet Cathay. They *zzzt, zzztt* here and there, hover stock-still in the air, then *zzztt*, fly backward, upside-down, or—oh no! Can it be true? Yes! Yes! The hummingbird just did a flying somersault! These tiny acrobats can reach speeds of sixty miles per hour. Each minute, they take about six hundred breaths and their oversized hearts beat up to twelve hundred times. However could your child get such an unpredictable creature to slow down long enough to let him watch it?

Well, of course, you know the secret that will allow your kid to watch a hummingbird up close. These little feathered beasts are so arrogant, so go-away-buddy-I-can't-be-bothered-with-you, that they're almost impossible to intimidate. You and your child can simply hang a hummingbird feeder outside a window. Paying you no attention, the hummingbird will go right on performing, gobbling up the sweet nectar, chasing away other hummingbirds, and zipping around like a small, colorful meteor.

You can buy a hummingbird feeder at any pet shop. Your child can prepare the nectar by boiling one cup of sugar and four cups of water in a pan on the stove until the sugar dissolves. Let it cool. Then fill up the feeder.

Once the birds find the nectar, your child can watch them for hours. And hummingbirds *do* stop: some have been seen perching quietly for half an hour. Except for perching, a hummingbird doesn't use his legs. It can't run, hop, or walk. Your child will also discover to his delight that these little flower kissers (as they're called in Portugal) do sing. Their high-pitched songs aren't very loud. But they know different songs and teach them to each other.

As your child contemplates these crazy characters with delight, he may also come to realize nature isn't always as "red in tooth and claw" as some poets have said. Often nature is quite happy and colorful like a rainbow.

How to Photograph a Hummingbird

If you already have some good photography equipment, you can teach your child to take a hummingbird's portrait. You'll need: a camera with a 200mm lens or a zoom lens of about 80 to 200mm; a tripod; and two to four remote flashes (which can be set up two feet or so from the feeder and fired from the camera). As a background for his photos, have your child place a sixteen-by-twenty-inch piece of white pasteboard two to four feet behind the feeder. Use film with an ISO of 64 to 100. Faster films will lose the fine details and the bird's vivid colors. The electronic flash is essential. The speed of the flash (not the speed of the shutter) determines the sharpness of the image, including how well he'll photograph the little guy's wings.

27. How to Hang by Your Knees

Can't keep still all day . . . . I like adventures, and I'm going to find one.

—Louisa May Alcott, Cool Mom of *Little Women*

No one has more fun in the zoo than the monkey flying through the air from tree limb to trapeze. And no one has more fun on the jungle gym than the kid who can hang by her knees. Many kids are too scared to attempt this feat of derring-do. They're afraid they'll fall on their heads. But teach her a secret, and your kid will soon be dangling upside-down in your backyard, happy as a spider monkey.

The secret is this: Hanging from a bar by her knees is actually *easier* than hanging by her arms because her leg muscles are much stronger.

To teach your child how to hang by her knees, stand beside her so you can catch her if she does fall. Have her sit on the bar. Then have her slide her bottom over the edge, holding on with both hands (Fig. 1).

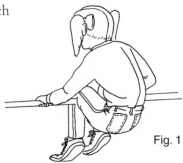

Fig. 1

Tell her to take her time. There's no rush. When she feels her knees firmly locked over the bar, it's time to ease herself down until her arms are straight (Fig. 2). Then she can let go with her hands (this is the scary part). And presto! She's upside down (Fig. 3).

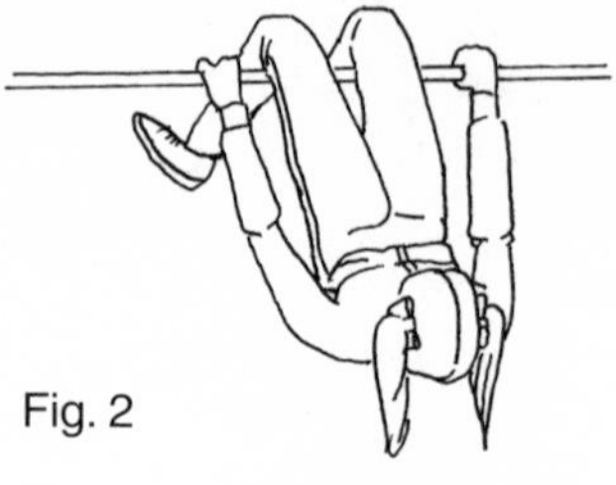

Fig. 2

Fig. 3

When she's ready to stop hanging from her knees, she simply reverses the process, curling her upper body toward the bar until she can grab the bar with her hands and pull herself up.

The adventuresome kid who learns how to swing from a bar by her knees becomes less afraid to take risks. And who knows? Later in life, she may discover that investing wisely in the stock market is a lot like hanging by her knees. She just needs to hold on until it's time to let go (and that really is the scary part).

28. How to Make Enough Clay for a Year

Art is the signature of civilization.
— Beverly Sills, Cool Mom of great opera

When a kid begins an art project, he hates to hear, "Oh dear, we don't have enough clay to make *that!*" You're certainly not about to let your child's enthusiasm wane for want of supplies. Puny chunks of plastic clay or Play-Doh only limit his imagination.

Fortunately, you know a way to free your kid's artistic talents so he can sculpt all the dinosaurs, space stations, and castles of his dreams. You know how to make enough clay for a year. The secret? It's all in the recipe. This clay recipe is a mom classic that's been around for generations. It's inexpensive. It bakes hard just like Play-Doh. It comes in every color of the rainbow. And it's so simple a kid can whip up giant batches for himself. Once he knows how, he can make as much clay as he pleases. But before he starts, make sure you have lots of salt—more salt than you've ever seen used in any recipe in your life.

First have your kid get out a pan—a BIG pan. Now, here's the recipe to follow:

6 cups of flour
2 cups of salt
8 tablespoons of vegetable oil
food coloring (all colors)
water

Have your child mix the flour and salt together. Then have him stir in the vegetable oil and add enough water (about two cups) to get the right consistency. If the clay is too wet, add more flour. If it's too dry, add more water.

Now he can divide the clay into chunks and color each chunk with food coloring. He can tint the clay all colors. Just tell him to go easy. A few drops of food coloring go a long way.

Once your kid can make his own clay, he can mold any statue he imagines. If he wants to keep his creation on permanent display, he can gently transfer it to a cookie sheet lined with aluminum foil. He can then bake the sculpture in a 225-degree oven until it hardens. Large pieces need to be turned over every fifteen minutes, so the bottoms can bake. He can also harden small pieces on paper plates in the microwave. Microwave the clay for one minute. Then check it every thirty seconds or so until it gets hard. Be forewarned, however: the microwave can cause the clay to become a bit puffed up.

By teaching your child how to make all the clay he needs for his creations, you're showing him how to depend on his own resources and to plan ahead. If he doesn't have enough clay to complete his project, he'll just have to make more. And next time, he'll make a bigger batch.

29. How to Identify Five Yucky Things Under a Log

Adventure is worthwhile in itself.
　　　　　　　　—Amelia Earhart, Cool Mom of aviation

Children are by nature of two minds. They're cheerful bundles of joy who love flowers, sunshine, and music. Then they'll suddenly pick up the nastiest, creepiest creature as if it were the dearest, sweetest pet on the planet and announce happily, "Mom, look what I found!"

So take your kid on a creepy, crawly expedition she'll never forget. Show her what's lurking under a log in the woods. Here are five slimy critters that should send adventuresome chills up her six-year-old spine:

Fig. 1

Earwig (Fig. 1): Hiding out in the very darkest, dankest bits of leaves and bark, this ugly little menace has a large, distinctive, hard "tail" that looks like forceps or tweezers. Contrary to popular myth, earwigs don't crawl into sleeping people's ears. They're also not poisonous. But that tail can inflict a painful pinch.

Scorpion (Fig. 2): A member of the spider family, this nasty fellow is yellow, brown, or black, and about the length of a new crayon. With pincers and a tail he usually holds over his back, he resembles a lobster. He hides under logs, eating centipedes, millipedes, wood lice, and spiders. But your kid may also occasionally find him in a dark place like a boot left on the back porch. Most types aren't poisonous to humans, but some are. So tell your child if she's ever stung by a scorpion, she must tell you immediately so you can get to a doctor.

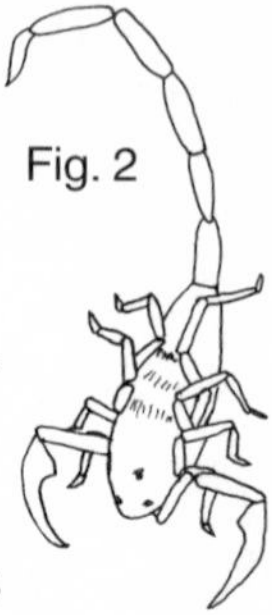

Fig. 2

Slug (Fig. 3): Just a snail without its shell. Formless, shapeless, and harmless. But if your kid touches it, she'll be slimed.

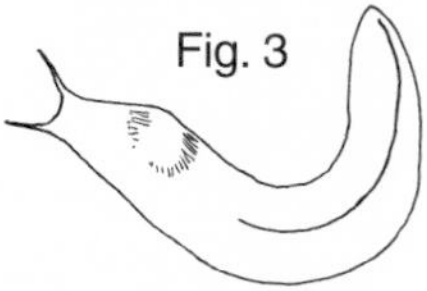

Fig. 3

Centipede (Fig. 4): Ranging from brown to dull orange with little black eyes at the tips of his antenna, this bad guy has about thirty or more legs. Unlike a slower-moving millipede (which has even more legs), the centipede moves fast and wriggles a lot like a worm. He's not poisonous, but his fangs can bite hard.

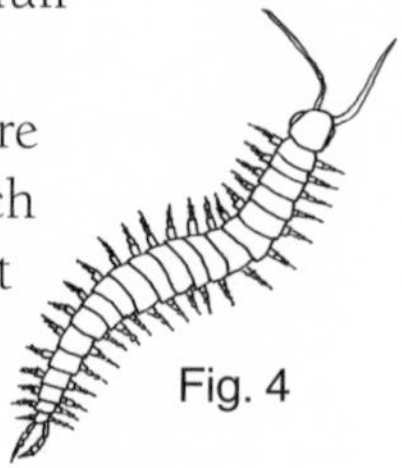

Fig. 4

Spider *Dysdera* (Fig. 5): Loves to eat wood lice (see box) and hides under logs just to dine. Resembles the brown recluse spider in that they both have six eyes. But *dysdera* has no violin marking on his back and he's not poisonous (see Secret 9, "How to Identify a Poisonous Spider"). Still, this spider can bite. So tell your child to satisfy her curiosity without picking him up.

Fig. 5

As your child learns to distinguish the dangerous critters under a log from the harmless ones, she'll also learn to adventure more safely. Paying attention to details will teach her how to be bold without being reckless.

COOL MOM FACT

The Happiest Under-Log Dweller

The good guy of under-log dwellers, the wood louse looks a bit like an armadillo. Also called a pill bug, tiggy-hog, or rolypoly, he rolls up so cutely into a ball when he's touched that some kids keep rolypolies as pets. A sow bug looks like a rolypoly, but here's the difference: The sow bug doesn't roll up in a ball. When touched, he'll run away.

30. How to Drive a Bumper Car

Enthusiasm is a divine possession.
    —Margaret S. Sangster, Cool Mom of American poetry

Driving a bumper car is like being a superhero. *Crash!* With bumpers of steel. *Bash!* With bullet-proof fenders. *Clang-bang!* The only difference is that a superhero always wins, but a kid driving a bumper car can get trapped in one place and smacked around by every passing pea brain.

When driving a bumper car, most kids head immediately toward the center of the action. Big mistake. That's where they're most likely to have lots of head-on collisions and get gridlocked. The secret to driving a bumper car adroitly is to drive as fast as you can on the outside of the track.

As your kid gets off to a flying start, he should race around the track, circling the other cars like a giant eagle searching for prey. Clue him into watching the other drivers' faces to see who looks most befuddled. Some drivers may even be driving the wrong direction. Once he spots a likely target, *wham!* Tell him to smash into the side of the other guy's car and send him spinning.

The second your kid scores a hit, he should quickly peel off—back toward the outside of the track—and immediately start scouting for another easy mark. Speed is important. The faster his pace, the harder he'll be able to hit. Yet even at their fastest, bumper cars move at such snail speeds no one gets hurt.

Driving a bumper car lets a kid work out his rough-and-tumble fantasies in a peppy, cheerful, spunky sort of way. At the same time, he may be absorbing a subtler lesson. Aggression paired with hostility becomes intolerable violence. But aggressive energy paired with high-spirited enthusiasm is a big key to success.

31. How to Get Gum Out of Your Hair (Without Scissors)

What do girls do who haven't any mothers to help them through their troubles?

—Louisa May Alcott, Cool Mom of *Little Women*

For some reason, girls are the master bubble-gum blowers of the universe. Some can blow a bubble the size of their heads. Trouble is, the better a kid gets at this feat, the likelier she is to wind up with an exploded bubble all over her face and sticky gum in her hair. Gum on her face can be removed by dabbing what's left of the chewed wad on her skin. But the more she pulls at the gluey mess in her hair, the more matted the gum gets. In another common occurrence, a kid will fall asleep at night with chewing gum in her mouth. Then she'll wake up in the morning with a glob stuck to the side of her head.

In such a crisis, most kids panic, believing they have only one choice: scissors. They think they have to whack out the gum and ruin the hair. But you know a way to remove the gum so your daughter can keep her long, silky tresses. The secret? Peanut butter. Oil in peanut butter breaks down the gum. A hefty dollop of peanut butter followed by shampoo and warm water will take that gum right out.

First, smear a generous glob of peanut butter over the gummy hair. Work in the peanut butter for three or four minutes until the gum feels less sticky. As the gum gets creamier, continue to work the peanut butter around each strand of hair.

Once the gum starts to fall into pieces, head for the sink. Shampoo your child's hair with lots of soap in warm water. Soon both the gum and peanut butter will just melt away, and your child will be giggling about being a "peanut head."

With no bother or fuss, you've just turned what could have been a disaster into a happy adventure. You've also taught your child that the first and most obvious solution to a problem isn't always the best. In the middle of a crisis, she should pause and think calmly. There's usually more than one way out of a sticky situation.

COOL MOM TIP

The Cool Mom Ice Trick

If you're fresh out of peanut butter, take an ice cube and rub it over the gum until it's frozen solid. Then crack the gum right off the hair, much as if it were hard taffy.

32. How to Build a Leaf House

This is the house that Jack built.
        —Mother Goose, Cool Mom of nursery rhymes

A pile of colorful leaves on a brisk autumn day beckons to a child's five senses. He wants to hear those crispy leaves crackle under his feet, crunch them in his hands, smell their smoky scent, gaze on their vivid hues. He literally wants to taste those autumn leaves.

As good luck would have it, you know just the way your child can immerse himself in all that natural beauty and remember it forever. You know how to build a leaf house. The secret lies in the way he places the twine that creates the house's framework. Just give him a big ball of twine and some newspapers. Then turn him loose to follow these steps:

1. Tie a twelve-foot piece of twine from a strong tree limb (about four feet in the air), as shown (Fig. 1).

2. Drive a stake in the ground about eight to ten feet from the tree. Tie the other end of the twine to the stake. This is the house's ridgepole.

3. On both sides of this ridgepole, make a tent-like structure by driving a series of little stakes in the ground, then

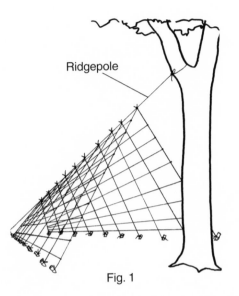

Ridgepole

Fig. 1

tying twine to these stakes. Place the stakes about one foot apart and three to four feet out on each side of the ridgepole, as shown.

4. Tie pieces of twine from one end of the structure to the other to create a cross-hatch pattern, as shown.

5. Lay sheets of newspaper over the twine. The newspaper will support the leaves, keeping them from falling through the twine structure.

6. Cover the frame completely with leaves, starting at the ground and working up to the ridgepole.

7. As a final touch, he should lay a few sticks or boards

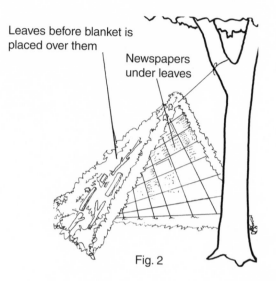

Leaves before blanket is placed over them

Newspapers under leaves

Fig. 2

against the leaves to keep the wind from blowing them away. Now he can fold an old blanket (or plastic tarp) across the ridgepole of the house. The blanket will keep all the leaves in place—and keep everyone who sits inside toasty warm. If he wants, he can now fix up the house on the inside, by covering the floor with a soft sleeping bag. He can even put in a pillow.

Your child and his friends can play many magical games in a house made of leaves. And after they're done, they can scoop up the leaves, put them in plastic bags, and set them out for the garbage man. Your child will have found a special way to drink in all of nature's beauty, and guess what? You'll have the autumn yard work done for another year.

33. How to Hop a Log on a Bike

I always say nothing you can imagine is totally impossible. It might be unlikely, but that's as far as I'll go.
                    —Emily Rodda, Cool Mom of *The Pigs Are Flying*

For kids who start mountain biking, rocks and logs seem like invincible obstacles. You need a flat level surface to ride a bike, right? Bikes can't fly over rocks and logs, right?

Right, but a bike can hop over them.

A bike can *hop?* Your child looks perplexed. *Don't be silly. That's impossible.*

But as a Cool Mom, you don't teach the impossible. Besides, you know a secret. A bike goes over any obstacle only one wheel at a time. That's all your child needs to be able to handle: one wheel at a time.

To teach your kid this classic skill, have her start by hopping a board about four inches across and one or two inches high. That way, if she fails to do the hop correctly, it's okay. She won't hurt herself. Teach her to ride the bike at a slow speed directly (straight-on) toward the board. When she's less than a foot from the board, she should stop pedaling and put the pedals in the three and nine o'clock positions (horizontal with the ground). Then she should push down on the handlebars and pedals. Now immediately have her yank up on the handlebars, pulling the bike up underneath her. To draw the bike higher and increase the springing motion, have her bend her knees and elbows. This action will cause the front wheel (the only one she needs to think about right now) to move up and over the board. As the front wheel clears the board, she should lean forward and, using her toe clips, yank up on the pedals with her feet. This lifts the back wheel up and over the board.

Once your kid can hop one board, place another board on the pile, then another and another. Once she knows how to do this trick, she can use it to hop a log on a mountain trail. She can also use it on a city street to hop a railroad track, a pothole, or a curb.

As your kid learns to hop an obstacle on her bike and lands safely on the other side, grinning from ear to ear, she may also be learning that she can overcome other difficulties, if she'll only apply a little thought and imagination. On the road of life, we all encounter obstacles we need to hop over.

COOL MOM TIPS

Safety Tips

When hopping a log on a mountain bike, your child should not turn the handlebars as she jumps (very important). The log also cannot be any thicker than the distance from the ground to the bottom of her chain wheel. If she comes upon a log bigger than that and she's not sure she can hop it, she should dismount and carry her bike over the log.

34. How to Carry a Football

When you've been given the football to carry, you've been asked to get the gold shipment through the badlands. So hold on tight and run as fast as you can.

—Cool Mom saying

Kids have little hands and small arms. When they try to carry a football, trouble erupts. Most kids will try to carry the ball clutched to their chest with both hands. Or they'll try to cradle it like a baby on one arm. Either way, when they're tackled or even bumped, they fumble the ball more times than they hold onto it.

Fortunately, there is a secret that will help your fledgling quarterback or running back carry the ball for big gains time and time again. He should create a "pocket" in which to carry the ball. By creating a pocket with the side of his chest, his upper arm, and his armpit, he'll prevent lots of fumbles.

First, have your child pick up the ball. Tell him that when he's running plays to the right, he should carry the ball under his right arm. During plays to the left, the ball goes under his left arm. This way he can use his free arm to fend off tacklers.

Teach him to jam the rear point of the ball as high as possible into his armpit, lifted up against his chest. His forearm should rest just slightly below the midline on the ball. The palm of his hand and fingers should be curled around the front point. Have him wiggle the ball around in this position until he finds a comfortable "pocket" in which the ball rests firmly but without tension.

Once he's got the right feel for the pocket, have him run around the yard or park, cradling the ball. Have him zig-zag back and forth, quickly changing directions. He should become as comfortably alert with that ball tucked into his armpit as he would be delivering newspapers.

By showing your child how to carry a football correctly, you'll be teaching him a skill many other kids won't know. When he explodes into the end zone for yet another six points, he'll grin and give you a thumbs-up. And later, when he thinks you're not listening, you'll overhear him tell his friends, "I learned to play football from my mom. She's cool!"

35. How to Identify Wildflowers

A flower touches everyone's heart.
> —Georgia O'Keeffe, Cool Mom of American art

Wildflowers are bits of beauty cast in bunches about the countryside for us to find. Teach your child to give beauty a name. Teach her to identify some of the wildflowers she'll meet on a country walk.

A child who sees a plethora of blossoms in a meadow may wonder, "How could anyone name them all?" But you know a secret. A simple system for identifying wild flowers has been worked out by the National Audubon Society. By looking at the shape and color of the blossom, your child can begin to identify any flower she spots. This will give her some botanical authority and will set her on the road to enjoying wildflowers more completely.

Basically, the Audubon System, as found in the *National Audubon Society Field Guide to North American Wildflowers*, breaks all flowers down into five tell-tale patterns:

Simple Shaped Flowers—Your child will tend to see these flowers as individual blossoms rather than clusters. Violets, poppies, and lilies are good examples. Flowers with this pattern can have three to six petals but usually have just four or five.

Daisy and Dandelion-like Flowers—These flowers have many petals (shaped like little straps) often radiating out from a button-like center. At first glance, a dandelion looks more like a small powder puff than a daisy. But have your child look closer, and she'll see what appears to be a single "puff" is really many tiny petals shooting out like rays of the sun.

Odd-Shaped Flowers—Some flowers defy description. Because they look so unusual they're simply called odd. Irises, columbine, and lady slippers fit this pattern.

Elongated Clusters—Long masses of flowers like those on lupine, larkspur, and goldenrod fall into this group. The flowers can be tightly or loosely arranged on the stalk.

Roundish Clusters—These rounded masses of flowers often resemble tiny bouquets. Queen Anne's lace, yarrow, and milkweed fit this pattern.

Once your child figures out the flower's shape and notes its color, she can then look it up in the wildflower field guide to find its name. Certainly, your child will find her sojourns through field and meadow a curious adventure. But as she explores the secret way to make sense out of those many different blossoms, she'll also gain a more intelligent understanding of the world. When intelligence marries beauty, the offspring is wonder.

36. How to Fall Down Without Getting Hurt

To leap is not only to leap, it is to hit the ground somewhere.
—Elizabeth Bowen, Cool Mom of *The House in Paris*

Kids fall down a lot. Whether they're on the playground, soccer field, ice-skating rink, or just walking down stairs, they trip, flip, tumble, and crash. And falling down *hurts*.

But you know a Cool Mom skill that will make those landings less painful. It's a move in judo called a "breakfall." Many kids confuse judo with karate, which involves lots of kicks, whacks, and slams. But judo is more like professional wrestling as taught by Olympic gymnasts. It's about balance and leverage. A breakfall, as its name suggests, breaks a kid's fall. The kid who knows this move can fall from a height of several feet, hit a hardwood floor, and land flat on his back without getting hurt. It can be painful to *watch*, but it's painless to *do*.

Here's how this breakfall works. As the kid falls, at exactly the same time he hits the floor, he has to slap the floor with his hand and whole arm, from shoulder to finger tips. He should hold his arm at a 45-degree angle from his body (Fig. 1). The slap plus the 45-degree angle work together to absorb most of the energy from the fall, spreading it over a large area, so the kid doesn't get hurt.

Obviously, you don't want your kid throwing himself down stairs to learn this nifty move. Instead, he can practice just by lying on his back and slapping the floor. One day, when he suddenly finds his feet slipping out from beneath him (again), he'll automatically go into his "judo move." To your great relief, he'll just get up, dust himself off, and keep smiling.

By mastering this skill, your child will learn that falling hurts less than the fear of falling. It's often said in judo that a kid can never win until he's not afraid to fall. That may also be true in life.

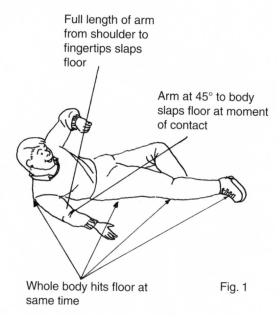

Full length of arm from shoulder to fingertips slaps floor

Arm at 45° to body slaps floor at moment of contact

Whole body hits floor at same time

Fig. 1

37. How to Pick Up a Kitten

I have just been given a very engaging Persian kitten . . . and his
opinion is that I have been given to him.
        —Evelyn Underhill, Cool Mom of contemplative prayer

In a well-mannered world, a child who has been given a kitten would think, "Got to be cool about this—stay calm." Then she would look the giver in the eye and very quietly say, "Thank you. It's exactly what I wanted." But no child ever responded in such a well-mannered way. The first words out of a child reflect exactly how she feels. "Wow! A kitten! He's so cute. Let me hold him. Gimme, gimme, gimme." Then she grabs at the kitten, which can hurt it badly and throw the poor little animal into a state of confusion.

Fortunately, you can easily teach your child to pick up a kitten in a way that it feels happy and safe. First, tell your child she should never pick up a kitten by the skin or the scruff of its neck. Being hoisted off the floor into the air many times its own height and dangling free makes a kitten quite anxious.

Instead, teach your child to place one hand under the kitten's chest just behind its front legs. She should avoid squeezing too tightly. The bones in a kitten's rib cage are fragile. Too much pressure can seriously injure the kitten. Next, have her slide her other hand under the kitten's hindquarters to support the animal's weight. Then she can lift. The kitten should be firmly cradled in both hands as your child brings it in against her chest.

If the kitten squirms and wriggles to get free, teach your child to hold the kitten with one hand, letting it lie along her forearm and snugly against her chest. Then have her cover the kitten's eyes and ears with her free hand. The little cat will calm down.

At the same time your child is learning how to pick up a kitten, she's also learning to be gentle with a creature smaller and weaker than herself. The kitten will reward your child's tender love with a rumbling purr, and you won't have to say a word. Just by its sweet response, the kitten is teaching your child to be kind.

COOL MOM TIPS

When a New Kitten Gets Homesick

If a new kitten wakes up crying in the night, this means he's homesick. Have your child put a ticking clock in the kitty's bed. The ticking will remind the baby cat of his mother's heartbeat. Your child can also wrap a soft towel around a hot water bottle (heated to about 102° F) and place it in the kitten's bed. The warmth will help remind the kitty of his siblings.

38. How to Play Better Soccer

You don't just luck into things . . . you build step by step whether it's friendships or opportunities.

—Barbara Bush, former First Lady and Cool Mom of six

Your child's an okay soccer player. But he wants to be better. He thinks the coach won't notice him. He's afraid he'll be benched.

Can you do anything to relieve his anxieties and help him play better? Absolutely. Show him a smooth move that any coach will notice. Teach him to do the "Dreaded Nutmeg." If he does this move in practice, he'll get all the attention he wants.

This play requires the "nutting" of one of your kid's opponents. When he "nuts" an opponent, he pushes the ball between the other guy's legs, then joyfully runs around behind the guy to collect the ball on the other side. For the open-stanced opponent, it's a nightmare. But the coach will notice and think your kid's pretty slick.

To do the nutmeg, your child should watch for an open-stanced player on the other team. The best defense, of course, is for the other guy to keep his legs together as your kid approaches with the ball. But it's hard to keep one's balance with both feet together, so many kids keep their legs splayed. By staying alert, your kid will catch an opponent with his feet unusually wide apart. This is his golden opportunity for a nutmeg.

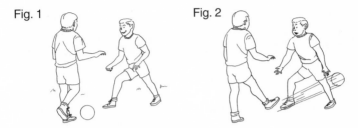

Fig. 1   Fig. 2

As he approaches his opponent (Fig. 1), he should look for the moment when the guy's legs are far enough apart to get the ball through. Then go for it! Have him knock the ball (without too much force) through his opponent's legs (Fig. 2). A nutmeg can be tough to execute. But when it works, he should run quickly around behind his opponent to collect the ball. If his opponent is moving to the right, your kid should run around to the left, and vice versa.

The nutmeg makes a kid look great in his coach's eyes. It also teaches him a lesson. The best soccer players aren't always the fastest or most agile. They're often simply those who've taken the extra time to think ahead and figure out some smart moves. Then they stay alert for the opportunity to make those moves happen.

COOL MOM TIP

Throughout this move, it's important for your child to smile at all times. And remind him that no nutmeg is complete until he cries, "Nuts!" as he rounds his embarrassed opponent to collect the ball.

39. How to Act Around a Horse

Things like confidence matter to horses, and they let you know if you don't have enough of it.
—Zilpha Keatley Snyder, Cool Mom of fantasy books

The horse is a timid giant. He did not come into this world as a fighter. God gave the elk his horns, the cat his claws, and the bee his sting. But he originally gave the horse only the power to run fast. It took centuries for the horse's soft toes to turn into hard hooves, which he can use as kicking weapons. Meanwhile, when he was still timid prey, the horse became man's friend and was bred up to have a large, muscular body. The result: an animal as timid and skittish as a rabbit with the muscles of a Clydesdale.

The trouble is, when kids get around a horse for the first time (often on vacation), they get so excited they go all to pieces. They run, yell, act silly, throw balls, slam gates—and spook the horse, who's then apt to kick or bite. So teach your child the secret of behaving properly around a horse: Never do anything suddenly.

When approaching a horse, your child should always move slowly and talk calmly. Remind her that a horse's eyes are on the sides of his head. This means he can see behind his rump as easily as he can see straight ahead of him. So even when your child approaches a horse from behind, she has to be careful. If she leaps down from a fence ten feet behind him, he can still see her, get scared, and kick with those powerful legs.

Most horses are gentle sweethearts. But a few are so ornery and contrary they'll kick and bite even when approached correctly. So caution your child never to approach a strange horse without first asking its owner about the animal's personality—how gentle he is, what he likes and dislikes, what he fears.

Horses are a lot like people that way. Although kids should avoid strangers until they're known to be friendly, the vast majority are warm, trustworthy, and loving.

40. How to Use a Carpenter's Brace

This, my friends, is progress's rule: Teach your child to use a tool.
—Cool Mom saying

When a kid picks up a carpenter's brace, he might think, *What a funny looking tool! But it looks like it's got a real purpose. I'll bet it's used for tightening bolts or something like that.* Wrong. It's actually used for drilling holes, and it's a tool that has been a major force in the history of Western progress. Being familiar with the ideas embodied in a brace is the best way to ensure the continuation of that progress. So teach your child a part of his culture. Teach him to use a brace and bit. Even a five-year-old can learn how.

As he's learning, have your child practice on a one-inch-thick piece of soft wood (like pine) clamped to the edge of a bench.

First, have him choose a bit (a screw-shaped piece of metal that bores the hole). To drill just any hole, any size bit will do. But if your child wants to drill a specific-sized hole, show him the little numbers stamped on each bit. The number tells (in sixteenths of an inch) how big a hole the bit will drill. An 8 means it will drill a hole 8/16ths (or half an inch) wide.

So how does he drill a hole with the bit? He needs leverage to get the job done. That's why the brace was invented—to give his muscles the added power of leverage.

First, have your child insert the bit into the brace by unscrewing the screw sleeve, which opens the jaws (Fig. 1). He can then tighten the jaws around the bit by tightening the screw sleeve. Now he'll place the tip of the bit smack in the center of the hole he wants to drill. If he's big enough, he should steady the brace against his body. If not, have him kneel on the bench (to get a good grip on the brace handle). Then you can steady the brace yourself as he cranks the handle to bore the hole.

At some point, he may hit a hard spot in the wood. Or his arms may be too short to fully turn the handle. That's the time to show him how to use the brace's ratchet action. Just have him turn the ring (Fig. 1). This changes the rachet action to clockwise or counterclockwise, whichever way he wants the bit to go. With a little back-and-forth ratchet action, he should be able to get the brace working again. Before long, he'll see the bit

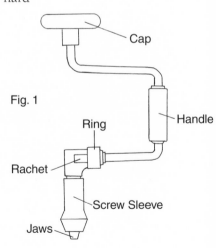

Fig. 1

Cap

Handle

Ring

Rachet

Screw Sleeve

Jaws

peeking through the bottom of the wood; and Yea! He's drilled a hole. It's a skill even many grown men never learn.

As your child grins with delight over his victory, you'll realize you've just empowered him to use one of the great tools of civilization. And that's not bad for a kid who's only five.

COOL MOM TIP

How to Avoid Splinters

A brace-and-bit often leaves tiny splinters at the bottom of the hole. Your child can prevent splinters in two ways:
1) When he first sees the bit emerging on the bottom of the wood, have him stop boring, turn the wood over, and finish off the hole neatly by boring in from the other side; or
2) Clamp a piece of scrap board to the bottom of the board he's drilling.

41. How to Treat a Bee Sting

Few creatures so tiny have managed to raise such unreasoning panic.
—Mary Webb, Cool English mom writer and poet

Many kids call any insect with wings and a stinger a bee. But bees or honeybees aren't the only stinging insects. Others include wasps, hornets, yellow jackets, and fire ants. If your child is stung by any of these nasty creatures, she'll usually come running to you. But what if she's stung while at school, at a friend's house, or on a camping trip? Or what if she's babysitting a baby brother who stumbles onto a hornet's nest?

Before such a crisis occurs, teach your child what to do if she or another child is ever stung. The big secret she should remember is this: Don't panic. By staying in control and following a few simple steps, she'll be safe. Soon the bite will stop hurting.

If your child sees a little black dot in the bite mark, this means the stinger is still in her skin. (This happens only with a honeybee.) If she sees a stinger, she should *not* pull it out. If she does, she could release more venom. Instead, she should scrape out the stinger with a blunt-edged object like a credit card or library card.

After the stinger comes out, have her wash the skin with soap and warm water.

Then have her take some meat tenderizer and add water to

make a paste. Tell her not to add too much water. She wants a paste, not a liquid. Have her rub the paste on the bite with a cotton ball. Then cover it with a Band-Aid. If she has no meat tenderizer, she can hold an ice cube against the sting for ten minutes to prevent swelling. Then she can soothe the skin by applying a paste of baking soda and water for twenty minutes. If the sting still hurts, it's okay to take acetaminophen (such as Tylenol) to kill the pain.

Allergies to bee, wasp, or yellow jacket stings are rare. Only about two in one hundred kids have allergic reactions. But should your child develop red, lumpy, itchy patches on her skin, an upset stomach, dizziness, or a tight feeling in her throat, she should call you or a doctor.

A kid home alone should also call 911 immediately if she or another child is ever stung in the mouth. Even without an allergic reaction, a sting in the mouth can quickly cause severe swelling. This, in turn, can block the airways so a child can't breathe.

Fear magnifies pain. By teaching your child what to do if she's ever stung by a bee, you're letting her know that even when you're not there, she should not be afraid. Knowing how to handle herself in a difficult situation gives her a sense of control. And that sense of control, in turn, reduces stress, eases pain, and builds self-confidence.

42. How to Hit a Baseball Farther

A hit that stings is a hit that stinks.

—Cool Mom saying

It's April, and a few days ago your kid took up baseball with a green-spring passion. Now his interest has suddenly waned. When you ask why, he complains that whenever he hits the ball, the bat stings his hands. He's getting no distance on his drives. He's about ready to pack it in.

Fortunately, you know a way he can turn his sting of defeat into the glory of victory. Soon he'll be hitting line drives and long, hanging fly balls that heart-throbbingly wait to drop for doubles and triples. That's because you know how to help him find the "sweet spot" on the bat.

The sweet spot is the location of authority. It's where weak bloopers are transformed into majestic fly balls. New York Giants manager Leo Durocher once said, "There are only five things you can do in baseball—run, throw, catch, hit, and hit with power." Finding the sweet spot on his particular bat will allow your child to hit with power. When hit with this power point on the bat, that little white ball will sail for its greatest distance.

First, teach your child how to find the sweet spot. Have him grip the bat the way he normally holds it when he swings.

Then without moving his hands, have him hold the bat straight out in front of him horizontally. With a rubber mallet, a hammer wrapped in a towel, or another bat, tap the bat along its full length. Almost every time you tap, your child will feel the bat vibrate in his hands. When he hits a ball on any of these vibrating spots, he's hitting with less than his full power.

But—and this is the really important *but*—at some point he will feel nothing at all. Nothing. The bat will just rest in his hands, solid and unperturbed. He has located the sweet spot. When he hits a ball on this place, he's hitting with his full power. Mark the spot with a piece of chalk.

Now toss your child a few pitches. Each time he swings, he should try to hit the ball on that chalk mark. Gradually, as he masters this lesson, he'll start clobbering the ball. His contribution to his team will soar.

And who knows? As the years go by, he could grow from a star Little Leaguer into a shining competitor in anything he chooses—all because you taught him it's not those with the most raw power who do the best in life, it's those with the most insight.

COOL MOM TIP

The sweet spot your child locates is good only for this particular bat held in the grip he normally uses. If he changes to a new bat or alters his grip by moving his hands up or down on the bat, the sweet spot will move and he'll have to locate it again.

43. How to Get Back into a Canoe (After You've Fallen Out)

Canoes don't act like they ought'er / When they tip over in the water.
— Cool Mom rhyme

Because it's so light, a canoe is fun to paddle on the water. It responds to the slightest touch. But this lightness can become a problem if a kid ever falls out. The child who falls (or jumps) overboard will be surprised how easily the canoe tips as she tries to clamber back in. Everybody in the canoe can wind up in the water, too—unless you know the secret that will help her get back into the canoe without tipping it over.

The secret is this: Any paddler who's still in the canoe (hopefully, this will be you) needs to act as a counterbalance. Then the one in the water can hoist herself over the side and back into the canoe.

Naturally, your child is wearing a life jacket. She's not about to drown. So there's no panic. Every move can be made slowly and methodically. First, have her hand you anything she's holding (like her paddle), so you can put it back in the canoe. Now move to the side opposite the one your kid is going to come over. Then have her boost herself up over the side of the canoe by grasping the gunwales (the sides of the canoe) with both hands. She should place one hand on the gunwale farthest from her and the other hand on the gunwale nearest to her. Tell her not to raise her body too far above the gunwale. That can cause the canoe to tip over again. She'll be back in the water, and you might be, too. Just have her hoist herself and sort of roll in over the gunwale.

As your child learns this worst-case-scenario skill, she's also learning that when you work together as a team, you can achieve far more than you could ever accomplish alone. Getting back into a canoe can be a bit harrowing. But later your adventure will be retold so many times it will attain the status of family legend.

COOL MOM TIP

What if You're Both in the Water?

If both you and your child are in the water, you can swim around the canoe and move to the side farthest from your child. Then you can act as a counterbalance to stabilize the canoe as she gets in. Once she's in the canoe, she can provide counterbalance while you hoist yourself out of the water and roll up and over the gunwale.

44. How to Track a Squirrel

If I had influence with the good fairy who is supposed to preside over the christening of all children, I should ask that her gift to each child in the world be a sense of wonder so indestructible that it would last throughout life.

—Rachel Carson, Cool Mom of the modern environmental movement

In his heart, every kid imagines himself as Davy Crockett or Frank "Bring 'em Back Alive" Buck, stalking a wild beast through the forest to its lair. But when he tries tracking a real animal—say, a squirrel—through your local park or backyard, the tiny rodent weighs too little to leave a clear track. Even if a kid manages to spy one squirrel track in the dirt, he's unlikely to find a second.

But you know a way your kid can track a squirrel to its nest tree every time: Do it in the snow. That's when a squirrel's tracks become as visible as a human's signature on white paper.

First, show your child what a squirrel track looks like. Have him notice that when a squirrel hops or gallops, his tiny front feet land first. These front feet or hands have four sharp-clawed toes and a very tiny "thumb" (which doesn't show up in the track). Once the squirrel's tiny "hands" touch the ground, his larger back feet hop outside and *around*, landing in front (Fig. 1). Since the squirrel's larger hind feet always land in front of his much smaller hands, your kid can tell in an instant which direction the squirrel was hopping. The squirrel in Figure 1, for example, was traveling north.

Once your child spots a squirrel track, he can tell whether it's a grey or a red squirrel by measuring the width of the track (A) with a tape measure. The grey squirrel, being larger, leaves a trail about four to six inches wide. A red squirrel's trail width is about three to four inches. The red squirrel's front foot width (B) will also be slightly smaller than the grey squirrel's.

A rabbit's track is often confused with a squirrel's track, but here's the difference: The squirrel's tiny front feet land side by side. When the rabbit hops, his front feet land one in front of the other.

As your child tracks a squirrel through the snow, he's learning to pay attention to tiny details many others don't see. And this ability to pay attention will make him feel closer not only to the squirrel, but also to himself. Many people spend much of their lives in a daze, as if they're half asleep. Staying alert to nature's tiny details wakes us up to ourselves.

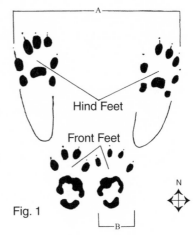

Fig. 1

113

45. How to Make a Snow Angel

Angels come in all sizes and shapes and colors, visible and invisible to the physical eye. But always you are changed from having seen one.

—Sophy Burnham, Cool Mom of angel books

The first snowfall has arrived. A sprinkling of soft powder covers the ground like baker's sugar. There's not enough white stuff to build a snowman or a fort. Yet your moppet still wants to make something in the snow.

Is this a problem? No! You know how even a two-year-old can create a personalized "art work" with almost no snow at all. She can make a snow angel. It's so easy it takes less than a minute.

When most kids first hear about a snow angel, they picture a snowman with giant white wings. Easy? They think it's the equivalent of trying to sculpt a statue of the Archangel Michael. But the snow angel you're talking about is the kind your kid makes lying down.

Just get your child snugly bundled up with mittens, boots, scarf, and cap. Then find a nice powdery patch of snow and have her lie down in it on her back. Now with her body still flat against the ground, have her wave her arms up and down, her legs open and closed, as if she were doing jumping jacks. As soon as she creates a deep indentation in the snow, have her stand up very carefully. She needs to stand up without breaking the outline of the silhouette she's just created. Have her step carefully away from the place where she was lying and look down. There—in the snow—is the perfect outline of an angel. On a sunny day, the angel may even glisten and shimmer in the sunlight.

If you have several children, they can all make angels in the snow to create an entire snow-angel family.

The angel will disappear as the wind blows or a new snowfall arrives. But long after the snow melts, your child will happily recall sculpting an angel with her own body. And this is only fitting and proper. Deep in our hearts, we know all children are little angels.

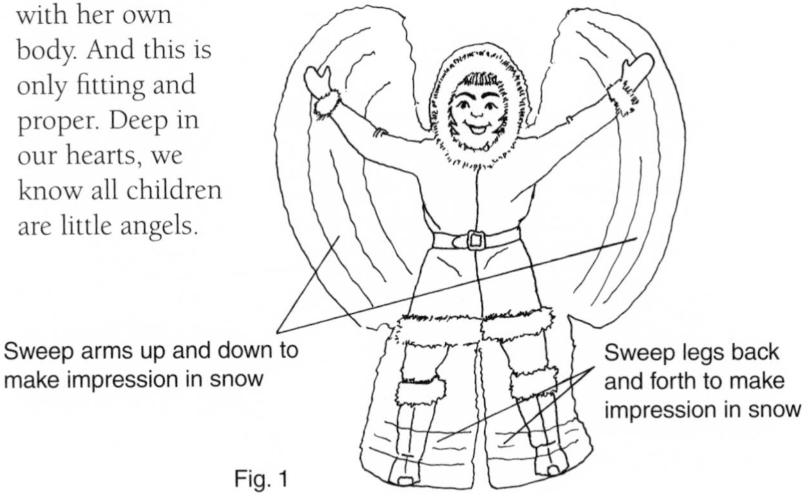

Sweep arms up and down to make impression in snow

Sweep legs back and forth to make impression in snow

Fig. 1

46. How to Use a Coping Saw

A person who can't use tools must feel like a Neanderthal in Homo sapien *clothing.*

—Cool Mom saying

Your child wants to put his name in raised letters on his room door. You think that's a great idea and suggest he cut the letters out of a one-inch-thick board. He protests that will be impossible as his name is Charles (or Sam or Chris), and saws only cut straight lines. How's he going to make the *C* and the *S*? And to manage the *A*? Why, with that little triangle inside, he'd have to be a genius.

Fortunately, as a Cool Mom, you know that what looks like genius is often simply a matter of finding the right tool. So tell him about the coping saw and show him how to use it.

The coping saw (Fig. 1) is one of the great tools of all time. Its secret is this: The height of its blade is about the same size as the width of the cut it makes. It can turn almost at right angles in its own cut. With a coping saw, your child can cut along almost any line he can draw. He can also cut that little triangle-shaped hole out of the *A* without cutting its legs off. But the thin blade of this saw does have one drawback. If used carelessly, it can crimp and be permanently damaged. It can also overheat and break. That's why it's important for your child to use a coping saw correctly.

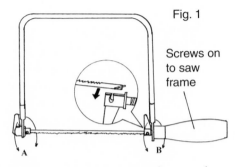

Fig. 1

Screws on to saw frame

First, have your kid draw the letters on the board he wants to cut. Then have him lock the board in a vise. If you don't have a vise, he can cut the wood without one, but it will be a lot harder.

Once the board is secured in the vise, have him start sawing. Remember, the coping saw cuts on the pull stroke, not on the push stroke. As he cuts, tell him not to twist the saw too much or it will break. As he saws around any curves (such as those in the letter *S*), be sure he keeps the blade moving back and forth. Tell him to change directions gradually as he saws. A sudden 90-degree turn could break the blade. To keep the blade from overheating and give it a chance to cool, have your child stop sawing once every minute or so.

When it's time to cut out that little triangle in the *A*, have your child follow these steps:

1. Drill a small hole in the middle of the triangle (see Secret 40, "How to Use a Carpenter's Brace").

2. Unscrew the wood handle of the saw.

3. Take the blade off the saw and put it through the drilled hole.

4. Reconnect the blade.

5. Screw back the wooden handle to tighten the blade.

By teaching your child to saw a curved line, you will open his mind to the possibilities of tools. Later in life, when others are looking for ways to quit on a sticky problem, he'll be looking for the right tools to solve it. He'll know that trying times are no time to quit trying.

47. How to Turn a Rowboat

I am not afraid of storms, for I am learning how to sail my ship.
        —Louisa May Alcott, Cool Mom of *Little Women*

The competent child can row a boat. But the really competent child can row a boat in more than one direction. When she wants to change directions in a rowboat, the competent kid quickly reverses her course. The boat wheels about to do her bidding.

What's the secret to turning a boat quickly? A maneuver called pivoting. With a pivot, your kid can turn the boat completely around and head back in the direction she came (which can be handy in an emergency). Or she can stop the boat partway through the pivot and head out toward a far distant shore.

First, teach your child to row straight ahead. The secret there is for her to brace her feet on the bottom ribs of the boat and pull back with equal force on both oars. Once she can row straight, have her pick out a new direction she wants to go. Tell her to pick out an object on the opposite side of the lake, then plan to turn the boat until it's aimed directly at that target. Let's say she picks out a dock to her left. As she watches the dock over her left shoulder, have her continue rowing straight with the right oar. But have her quickly and smoothly row backwards or "backwater" (see box) with her left oar. The boat will start turning smartly to the left.

If the target is to her right, she should watch it over her right shoulder and begin to backwater with her right oar. Remind your child to put the blades of both oars into the water at the same time and begin both strokes at the same time. When she finishes her stroke, she should raise both oars together out of the water.

Long before she's old enough for a driver's license, your child can learn to row a boat and handle a "vehicle" responsibly. If she makes a mistake, she's not about to run into anyone or have a major collision. But at the same time, she's learning to rely on herself to get where she wants to go.

COOL MOM TIP

How to Backwater

To backwater, your child should start with the oar handle in front of her chest. As she dips the blade in the water, have her push the handle away from her body. As she lifts the blade out of the water, she should pull the handle back toward her body, then dip the blade back in the water. She's now set for her next stroke.

48. How to Jump on In-Line Skates

There is only one proof of ability: action.
        —Marie von Ebner-Eschenbach, Cool Countess of Austria

Your kid knows how to in-line skate. He's good at keeping his balance, turning, stopping, and maneuvering up and down hills. But you figure it's time to add some spice to his in-line-skate life. It's time to teach him how to jump.

The secret: He needs to start small and build up as his confidence grows. First he needs to learn how to jump over a crack in the sidewalk.

Before the jump, he should build up his speed. Momentum will make the jump easier. About five feet before the crack in the sidewalk, he should start getting ready. He may be tempted to lift off with his stronger foot. But he'll get more lift—and stability—by lifting off with both feet at the same time.

When he's in the air, he should grab his boots with his hands, if only just for a second. This adds panache to the jump. It also forces him into a tight body position, which will increase his control.

As he jumps, your child should concentrate on his body balance (not his skates). Tell him to be ready to stride forward as soon as he hits the ground. As he lands on the other side of the crack, he should land with his stronger foot first. Once again, this gives him a larger base and makes him more stable. He should trust his instincts and stride forward with the foot he considers his strongest. Right footers—called "regular footers"—usually put the right foot in front. "Goofy footers"—a tag some skaters consider a mark of distinction—put their left foot forward. He can then end his jump with a glide.

Once your child can jump a sidewalk crack with flair, he can go on to a more difficult obstacle like a curb. But he shouldn't get impatient or overly ambitious. On skates, as in life, risk-taking needs to be tempered with acquired skills and good judgment. When in a delicate situation, always put your best foot forward.

49. How to Make Finger Paints

Life is a succession of moments. To live each one is to succeed.
                                    —Corita Kent, Cool Mom of graphic arts

From the time they're handed their first solid food, children become aware of squishing. They've been going along quite happily drinking milk from a cup and crunching on toast. Then one day they're handed a banana and *squish! Wow, that feels yucky, slimy, and shmucky. I LOVE IT!* From then on, they're hooked on squishing everything from mashed potatoes through their fingers to mud through their toes.

Eventually, your child will discover finger paints. And you know a secret she can use to make all the finger paints she needs: shaving cream. With one can of shaving cream, food coloring, and a few sheets of slippery paper, your child can satisfy her squishing urges for hours. Just squeeze six to a dozen dollops of shaving cream onto a paper plate or into an empty egg carton. You may want to tie a bib or a big thirsty towel around your kid's neck to keep the mess off her clothes. Then add different food colorings to each foamy dollop. Set out a bowl of water beside a piece of shiny white paper and turn her loose.

Now she can fingerpaint a picture of anything her squishy

little heart desires, from the dog chasing a Frisbee to a garden of roses. For even more fun, let her fingerpaint outside one warm summer day in her swimsuit. She and her friends can paint with their toes, their elbows, their knees. They can paint each other.

Once the art session ends, you can wash everyone up with a garden hose. The "paint" will leave your kid's hands soft and clean. And her paintings will smell as fresh as a laundered sheet hung out on the line to dry.

Fingerpaint art as a rule isn't made to decorate the walls of a room or a refrigerator door. It's meant to provide fun only for the moment. Sure, hard work is important. But a talent for goofing off in the moment is also a cool skill everybody should learn.

50. How to Build an Igloo

Nature has no mercy at all. Nature says, "I'm going to snow. If you have on a bikini and no snowshoes, that's tough. I'm going to snow anyway."

—Maya Angelou, Cool Mom of American poetry

Yes, they're from another culture. Sure, they look exotic. And, okay, they can withstand hurricane-force winds on an open plain. But anybody can build an igloo. Honest. If you live in a cold, wintry place (like Minnesota, Montana, or Maine), you and your child can build an igloo while playing in the snow.

You need only a snow shovel, a snow saw (a carpenter's saw will do just fine), heavy duty gloves, and the secret: deep snow so hard-packed it can support the weight of a heavy adult. The snow should be solid enough that it won't break when you pick up a big chunk.

Locate your future igloo on an open field or backyard where there's plenty of hard-packed snow. On the ground, scrape clear a circle ten to fifteen feet in diameter. Leave snow about three feet deep under the igloo.

Now saw a bunch of blocks about one-by-two-by-four feet in size. Carry the blocks to your igloo site. Place them around the edge of the cleared circle. Trim the bottom row of blocks to form a spiral ramp (Fig. 1). As the igloo grows taller, use smaller and smaller blocks. Slant each row of blocks farther in toward the center. The weight of the blocks will make the igloo stable.

Make a small entrance. Making it small will keep wind from blowing snow into the igloo. It will also keep out any stray polar bears that might be in your backyard. Dig a small trench in the snow from the inside, under the set-up blocks, to the outside (Fig. 2). Outside the entrance, set up two vertical snow blocks. Place another block across the top.

Dig out most of the snow under the floor of the igloo. This will give your kid extra head room. Move the last few blocks in through the entranceway.

Now close the dome. The dome won't collapse. But you can get extra insurance that it won't by propping up the dome blocks from inside with a stick. You can remove the stick later. Before closing the dome, clear away any snow that accumulated in the igloo as it was built.

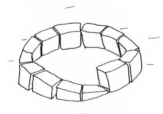

Fig. 1

Open to inside of igloo

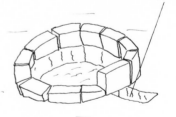

Fig. 2

Now stuff snow in the cracks from the outside and smooth the inside of the igloo. If the inside is one smooth surface, the snow won't drip as it melts. Cover the floor with some kind of camping mattress.

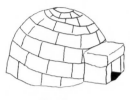

Fig. 3

And you're done (Fig. 3)! Within a few weeks, the heat your kid and his friends generate as they play in the igloo will turn the walls to solid ice.

A child who can build an igloo has learned he's not a victim of his environment. He's the master. With a little hard work, he can transform an aloof, forbidding land into a snug, safe shelter against the storm.

COOL MOM TIP

If the blocks you cut from the snow are still not quite strong enough to build with, set them out overnight to harden in the wind. A light spray of water from a squirt bottle should make those blocks icy hard by morning.

---

51. How to Catch a Firefly

Whenever a firefly blinks, somewhere a fairy laughs.

—Cool Mom saying

Fireflies, or lightning bugs, are the most enchanting of all beetles. Blinking on and off on a warm summer evening, they float in the darkness like dozens of twinkling stars come down to earth. Even more wondrous, their fire is not hot, but cold. So treat your eager explorer to a magical adventure she'll never forget. Teach her how to catch a jar full of fireflies—like a whole jar full of Tinker Bells—to set by her bed as a light against the night.

The secret is simple. She needs only a glass jar with a metal top. Have her use a hammer and a nail to poke air holes in the metal top. Now she's ready for a nocturnal adventure.

Once it's dark and the fireflies come out, have your child set her jar in a handy place on the grass and zero in on one insect. Have her wait for the firefly to flash. She should then walk to that spot and stand still. When the firefly blinks again, she can quickly put both hands over the creature. Most fireflies are so surprisingly slow, even a three-year-old can catch one. Have your child hold her hands up and peek inside to make sure the firefly has been trapped. Once she sees her little firefly friend blinking inside her hand, have her carefully transfer him to the glass jar. On a good night, a child can capture thirty, forty, or more fireflies in an hour.

Soon your child will have several dozen fireflies blinking in the jar. She can now take them home and keep them by her bed as she sleeps. As she snuggles under the covers, she'll feel closer to nature's mysteries. And the next morning, when she lets the fireflies free, she'll have gained a greater appreciation for the night. It's the only time you can catch fireflies.

52. How to Choose the Right Weight Bat

You have to make your own choices, and then live with them.
—Ilene Cooper, Cool Mom of *Choosing Sides*

Most kids think the bigger their baseball bat, the farther they'll hit. So they choose the biggest bat they can find. Unfortunately, the dragon-sized weapon they select is so heavy they can only swing it at a snail's pace. They miss all the fast pitches. The child looks less than his best simply because his bat is too heavy.

But you know how to help your child perform at his best. You know how to help him choose a bat that's not too heavy. Have him give it the weight test.

Here's how it works: Have your kid take his favorite bat and hold it out straight in front of him with both hands, arms fully extended. The bat should be horizontal with the ground. Start counting slowly to ten. If he tires or begins to tremble before you reach ten, the bat is too heavy. Have him choose a lighter bat and repeat the test. After a few tries, he'll find a bat that's the right weight.

Your child may worry that a lighter bat will keep him from being a slugger. That's not true. Remind him it's the speed of his swing, not the weight of his bat, that determines how far a hit ball will travel. Sure, if he builds up his muscles until he can swing a heavier bat equally fast, he'll hit the ball farther. But until he gets those muscles, he's better off using a lighter bat and swinging faster.

As he smacks out those hits in the season ahead, he'll also be learning another lesson. It's great to be ambitious and to have big dreams. But the person who knows his own strengths and limits is more likely to make those dreams come true.

COOL MOM FACT

What Happens when Bat Meets Ball?

When a Major Leaguer hits a fast ball squarely, the ball is being hit with eight thousand pounds—or four tons—of force. That's the equivalent of setting two family cars on the ball. For a split second, the ball squashes down to half its diameter. But it snaps back to its original size so fast you can't see it.

53. How to Do a Cartwheel

Hard work has made it easy. That is my secret. That is why I win.
—Nadia Comaneci, cool Olympic champion

Gymnastics promotes poise, physical confidence, and health to the body and mind. One of the most joyous of all gymnastic stunts is the sideways handspring, otherwise known as the cartwheel. Unfortunately, when most children try their first cartwheel, they look anything but agile. Their arms stick out at odd angles. Their knees bend. Their feet do an odd hippety-hop when they land. They resemble a Daddy Longlegs learning to walk.

But you know the secret to performing a cartwheel with grace and style. Have your child concentrate on getting her hips high in the air. Then have her envision her body as a giant wheel spinning over the ground. As she spins, tell her to keep her arms and legs wide apart but nice and straight.

Once she understands the secret, have her follow these steps:

1. Start with her hands in the air and feet wide apart like the spokes of a wheel. She should rest all her weight on her left leg and point her right toes in the direction she's going to spin.

2. She should reach out with her right arm and fall sideways to the right, shifting her weight to her right leg. Now, to get her hips high in the air she must kick up hard with her left leg just as she lands on her right hand. Catching herself first with her right hand, she should then spin like that giant wheel with her arms and legs straight at all times. Tell her to keep her motion fluid. She needs to touch the ground in this sequence—right hand, left hand, left foot, right foot—in one smooth, fluid spin.

If her legs arc over at first, that's okay. Just tell her to kick up with more energy and get her hips higher the next time. She may also need to spin faster. A cartwheel requires a certain aggressive enthusiasm. There's no such thing as a lack-adaisical cartwheel. If she does the stunt halfway, she'll look like that Daddy Longlegs. But with enough energy and practice, she'll soon be executing a cartwheel smoothly.

Doing this stunt with confidence gives a child a sense of body control, poise, and strength. It also suggests she needs to tackle even routine exercises with a winner's enthusiasm. Later in life, when challenged by a difficult job, she may remember how she felt doing a cartwheel and realize she needs to put more energy into the task. Halfway efforts produce halfway results. Full-hearted enthusiasm leads to full-blown success.

COOL MOM TIP

If your child has trouble getting her hips high enough, you can stand behind her. As she turns over, catch her waist and lift her hips to the correct position.

54. How to Pick Up a Budgie (or Any Small Bird)

What do we live for, if it is not to make life less difficult to each other?
—George Eliot (Mary Ann Evans Cross),
Cool Mom of the English novel

Budgerigars—"budgies," as we lovingly call them—are delicate. Under all those soft, fluffy feathers, they have vulnerable little bodies, and their teeny-tiny parakeet bones are hollow. Compared to a budgie, your child is a powerful giant. Even so, a budgie has a hard, pointed beak that can nip a child and make him afraid to handle it. So teach your child the way to pick up a bird that will make him and the budgie good pals. Teach him how to use the finger collar. By making a finger collar, he'll keep the budgie from pecking him and at the same time help the bird feel secure.

Before your child can pick up a bird, of course, he has to catch it. Some budgies are quite tame. Others flap wildly around in the cage. That's why the bird net was invented. A sort of miniature butterfly net, a bird net can be purchased in any pet store. Keep one by the cage.

Once the bird has been captured in the net (a fairly simple task), it's time for your child to apply the finger collar. As he reaches into the net, have him place the palm of his hand on the bird's back. Then have him slide his index and middle fingers forward, grasping the bird's neck and head between his two fingers (Fig. 1). This forms a collar that prevents the bird from turning its head and pecking.

Now your child feels secure. The bird, being firmly held, also feels secure. As an added advantage, your child can now pull the bird out of the cage without accidentally striking its head against the side of the door. It's a terrific all-around solution to an otherwise difficult problem.

As your child learns to handle the bird gently, he's also absorbing a second lesson that he might not recognize right away—that when you practice compassion, you discover the very heart of moral awareness, the ability to see another as one's self.

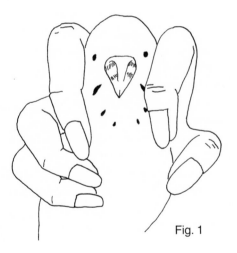

Fig. 1

55. How to Build a Really Cool Snowman

When I no longer thrill to the first snow of the season, I'll know I'm growing old.

—Lady Bird Johnson, Cool Mom of the White House

The first heavy snowfall always brings out a kid's ambitions. She wants to do something special. She envisions building a snowman the whole neighborhood will remember for years.

Well, of course, you know about a special type of snowman you and your kid can build that everyone will remember. It has a body of snow and a head of fire. You simply build a normal snowman—until you get to the head. Then you make the head out of a snow candle. When you light the candle, the snowman's whole head will glow.

First, make the snowman's body the usual way. Roll a small snowball across the yard until it becomes a giant ball. Do this twice—once for the base of the snowman, a second time for his chest. Where the snowman's shoulders would normally be, flatten the body on top.

Now it's time for you and your child to make the spectacular head. Make a bunch of small snowballs. Place seven or eight of these small snowballs in a circle on top of the flat shoulders. This will serve as a "foundation" for the head. Now using the other snowballs like bricks, build a circular wall three or four snowballs high (Fig. 1). With each layer of snowballs, slant the wall slightly inward, toward the center of the circle. Leave plenty of little holes between the snowballs. These holes will allow the heat to escape. That way, the snowman's head won't quickly melt from the heat of the candle inside.

Now begin sloping successive rings of snowballs to make a dome. At the very top of the tiny dome, show your child how to leave a hole just large enough for your hand. Now take a real wax candle and set it down inside the dome. Finish the snowman with two rocks for his eyes, a carrot for his nose, rocks for his mouth, and sticks for his arms. Come sunset, light the candle and cap off the snowman's head with one last snowball on top. Then stand back and admire your creation. With his body of snow and his glowing head, the whole snowman will seem to be made of fire and ice.

As your kid builds this really cool snowman, she's also learning a little lesson about innovation. There's nothing new about a snowman or a snow candle. But when two old ideas are put together for the first time, they suddenly create something new that's never been seen before. That's the essence of ingenuity.

Fig. 1

56. How to Win at Arm Wrestling

Arm wrestling is much more about speed and leverage than it is about strength. With good technique, I've seen 120-pound women drop 300-pound men.

—Mary McConnaughey, Cool Mom of heavyweight wrestling

All kids start out in life as seven-pound weaklings. And don't think they haven't noticed. Years after leaving the nursery, they still feel weak and wish they were strong. Wouldn't it be great to beat a really big guy at arm wrestling? Well, your kid can do just that. You know a secret that will help him. Spinach? No. But with this mom skill under his belt, he will feel like Popeye.

Here's the insight that will make your kid Arm-Wrestling Champ of the Western World (or at least the second grade): Beating someone at arm wrestling involves beating his wrist, not his arm.

Every arm-wrestling match starts with a friend shouting, "Ready, set, go!" The second your kid hears the *t* in "set," have him quickly curl his own wrist, pointing his knuckles back toward his own body. To get the most leverage, he should keep his arm as close to his body as possible.

As he curls his own wrist toward himself, he's also cocking

the other guy's wrist backward. By bending his opponent's arm at the wrist, he's destroying the other guy's ability to use his entire hand and arm for leverage. Before his opponent has time to think twice, Wham! Bam! Your kid has won.

If your kid wants to buff up before the big event, he can squeeze Silly Putty or one of those hand-muscle-strengthening balls sold in any sporting goods store.

As physical challenges go, arm wrestling is one of the least aggressive. Yet it keeps cowardly aggressors away. A kid with arm-wrestling prowess who feels and acts physically confident will be less likely to be bullied.

57. How to Tell How Far Away the Lightning Struck

A scientist . . . is not only a technician: he is also a child placed before natural phenomena which impress him like a fairy tale.
     —Marie Curie, Cool Mom of two Nobel prizes in physics

No child can go unimpressed by a thunderstorm. As lightning streaks across the sky, quickly heating the air around it to an explosive sixty thousand degrees, it makes a thunderous *CRAAACK!* that can capture the most blasé kid's attention and turn the bravest kid's knees to jelly.

But you know how to make a thunderclap more understandable and less frightening. You know how your kid can figure out for herself how far away the lightning struck. Once she realizes that great flash and loud *boom-itty-boom-boom* are five or six miles away, she'll have learned something new about nature, and she'll be less afraid.

Here's the secret: Light travels at a whopping 186,000 miles per second, so your child's eyes see the lightning the instant it flashes. But sound—which, of course, includes thunder— pokes along toward her ears so slowly it takes approximately five seconds to go one mile. Therefore, your child can tell how far away that lightning was just by timing how long it takes the thunder to arrive after she sees the flash.

Using a watch with a second hand, have your child count the number of seconds between the lightning flash and the thunder. Then have her divide by five. Her answer will be the number of miles away the lightning struck. Twenty seconds between the flash and the boom, for instance, means the lightning is four miles away.

Lightning can be dangerous, so a child should be alert. During a thunderstorm, she should stay away from wide grassy expanses (like golf courses), water, and tall trees. If she's outdoors during an electrical storm, she should also remove metal or conductive objects most people overlook, such as eyeglasses with metal frames, a helmet, or shoes with metal cleats. But as your child learns to judge danger for herself, she's also learning that whenever she's fascinated or afraid of something, she needs to learn more about it. Knowledge casts light on all our dark fears.

COOL MOM FACTS

- Low, rumbling thunder is farther away. High-pitched, crackling thunder means the lighting is much closer.

- When lighting strikes less than one hundred yards away, it makes a startlingly loud, high-pitched BANG! That's because the lightning is so close, its shock wave hasn't yet turned into thunder.

- The temperature of a lightning bolt is three times the temperature of the sun's surface.

- A lightning bolt can be as narrow as half an inch.

58. How to Recover a Fumble

There are two kinds of people in the world: those who complain about the way the ball bounces, and those who are already working hard to recover the fumble.

—Cool Mom saying

As leaves change to crimson and gold and pumpkins ripen in the fields, it's football season. Time for the power and glory of long bombs, touchdowns, extra points, heroic victories—and fumbles. Ah, sad but true, not every kid on the team wins cheers. Some fumble the ball and help their teams lose the game.

But your kid knows how to recover a fumbled football and help save the day. That's because you've taught him the secret: Forget about trying to grab the ball and run with it. Just smother that sucker with your whole body.

A football is so oddly shaped that once it hits the ground, it bounces as crazily as a jumping bean. A kid who dives to grab the fumbled ball with his hands can send it sailing into the waiting arms of an opponent. If he attempts to grab the ball, he may just slap it away. The important thing is to capture the ball.

So here's how your kid can capture that fumble with flair. First, remind him to be aggressive. He who hesitates is last.

He should run at the ball as fast as he can. Second, tell him to expect the ball to bounce all sorts of quirky ways. Never take his eyes off his prize.

Once he's above the ball, he should cover it with his chest. This chest-over-the-ball move offers two big advantages. One, he'll hide the ball from all those opponents streaking his way. Two, he'll be able to start forming a deep pocket with his body into which he can smother the ball.

He needs to scoop the ball up against his chest and cradle it with his arms, hands, and thighs. As he falls toward the ground, tell him to twist his body, so he'll fall on his side. (This keeps the ball from careening out of his arms as he hits the ground.) The instant he hits, he should fold his arms over the ball and draw his knees up under it, tucking his whole body around the ball in a fetal position. This knee-up position creates a deep, protective pocket for the ball. No one will be able to knock it loose or pry it away. The ball will belong to him. This position also protects his knee joints as the other players pile on.

As the referee unknots that pile of players and your kid emerges from the bottom with a grin, he'll know that staying alert pays. But as he holds the ball aloft as a sign of victory, he may also have learned another small life lesson: No game plan works perfectly. Fumbles happen. It's those with the resilience to recover and keep moving forward who eventually win.

59. How to Pitch a Horseshoe

People who like people like horseshoes.

—Cool Mom saying

Horseshoe pitching is a friendly competitive sport. You have no hot-dogging defender at the basket to block your child's best shot, no offensive offense to celebrate arrogantly in the end zone. It's the least intimidating of all games, which makes it perfect for relaxed moments of good sportsmanship between you and your child.

So what's the secret of success? Certainly stance, swing, and follow-through all count. But, as a Cool Mom, you know the single biggest secret is how your kid holds the shoe. Of all the grips, the most reliable is the one-and-one-quarter-turn heave (Fig. 1). This grip has won more world championships than any other.

To teach your child this grip of champions, first show her the calks (the little raised bits of metal on the bottom of

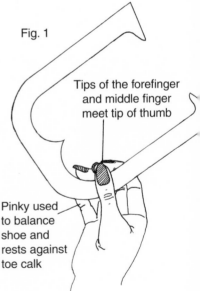

Fig. 1

Tips of the forefinger and middle finger meet tip of thumb

Pinky used to balance shoe and rests against toe calk

the shoe that keep a horse from slipping). Now have her grip the shoe (Fig. 1) with the calks pointing down. Her thumb, middle, and index fingers should meet at the tips, as shown, and her pinky should support the shoe for balance. The pinky along with her ring finger will also keep the shoe level as it's released. The thumb and forefinger release last.

When gripped and tossed correctly, a horseshoe will spin as it sails toward the stake. If it wobbles a little in flight, that's okay. A slight wobble can even help soften the landing so the horseshoe doesn't bounce wildly. Once your child has mastered this toss, she can enjoy playing horseshoes. Even if she's not winning, she'll know she's playing her best. If the horseshoe just lands close to the stake, that's worth some points. And one day, perhaps when she least expects it, *krrang-a-lang-a-lang*, she'll hit her first ringer. Wow! Pitching horseshoes is cooler than watching cartoons!

Learning to toss a horseshoe can take many unhurried hours. And as the two of you spend those long twilight evenings standing side by side, sailing pieces of iron through the warm summer air, you'll be fostering confidence and competence where it is best learned—in an arena of friends, an arena of mutual trust and respect.

COOL MOM TIP

When a child first tries to pitch horseshoes, she will usually grab the horseshoe by the curved end and point the open end at the stake. This is called the flip grip. The flip grip is a low-scoring toss. It's not a good idea to use it.

60. How to Hear a Falling Star

*If you don't succeed with Plan A, use Plan B. And always have a
Plan B. Plan Bs are the great secret to success.*

—Cool Mom saying

When some kids hear about an approaching meteor shower,
they get super excited. They can't wait to see falling stars. But as
the meteor-shower date approaches, sometimes black clouds
gather, rain falls in torrents, and the kid thinks he's out of luck.

Never one to give in to despair, you point out it's okay if
he can't see falling stars. He can listen to them instead.

Listen to a star fall? Sure. That's because you know the trail
behind a falling star leaves small particles—called ions—that
echo as "pings" from FM stations over the horizon. Your child
can pick up these pings on any good FM radio with an
FM/TV antenna. Even if he can't see any falling stars, listening
to their pings will give him an idea how many meteors fell
that night. Tuning into an FM station during the day can also
alert him to a shower that's going to be particularly active.

Many amateur astronomers use an FM radio tuned somewhere between 88 and 108 MHz and a Yagi FM/TV antenna.
The best frequencies to tune to are between 50 and 120 MHz.

146

During the shower, tune your receiver to a station located two hundred to one thousand miles away, one you seldom hear.

Suddenly, a meteor streaks through the stratosphere. The radio signal bounces off the meteor's ionized trail, hopping over the horizon, and treating you to a brief "ping." It might sound like a tone, a bit of music, a voice, or simply static. The sound will last for as long as the meteor trail lasts, usually from one hundred milliseconds to a few seconds.

As your child "listens" to meteors streaking overhead, he may also absorb another life lesson: Success doesn't come just to those lucky enough to be in the right place at the right time. If you have a backup plan, you can often create your own luck.

COOL MOM FACT

When Stars Fall in the Daytime

Some meteors fall only during the daytime. The International Meteor Organization lists a dozen daylight meteor showers that peak after sunrise and are followed almost exclusively by radio observations. Here they are:

Shower	Date	Shower	Date
Cap/Sagittarids	Jan 13–Feb 4	Arietids	May 22–Jul 2
chi-Capricornids	Jan 29–Feb 28	zeta-Perseids	May 20–Jul 5
Piscids (April)	April 8–April 29	beta-Taurids	Jun 5–Jul 17
delta-Piscids	April 24	gamma-Leonids	Aug 14–Sep 12
epsilon-Arietids	April 24–May 27	Sextantids	Sep 9–Oct 9
Arietids (May)	May 4–June 6	o-Cetids	May 5–Jun 2

61. How to Stand on Your Head

Could it be that people standing on their heads have it right and the rest of us have it upside down?

—Cool Mom saying

Standing on one's head may seem simple enough to you. But to a child who's been walking around only a scant few years, a headstand sounds like a revolutionary achievement. She's finally gotten good at standing on her own two feet, running, and jumping. Suddenly, the idea of standing on her noggin seems like an exciting alternative. It's also another victory in balance.

But how, she wonders, can anybody stand upside down on a head that's so roly-poly? She may keep falling over backwards until she gets so tired she just quits. That's bad. Cool Moms don't teach quitting. So teach your child the headstand secret that will make her balance like an Olympic gymnast: Tell her about the tripod.

Creating a tripod with her two arms and her head gives her upside-down body the stability of a pyramid. It also allows her to distribute her weight evenly, so she won't put all her weight on one hand or her neck. To create the tripod, she should simply bend over and position her head and hands as

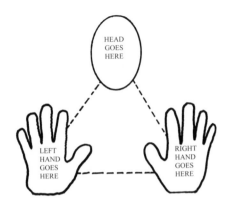

shown above. Her three spots of contact with the floor should form a triangle. Then have her lift one foot in the air until it's straight above her head. Help her position her foot properly by holding it in the air. Now have her kick up with her second foot. As she does, catch that foot, too. Hold both feet together until she's perfectly balanced. Then let go.

After a few tries, she can start practicing on her own. Eventually, with enough perseverance, standing on her head will become as natural as standing on her feet.

The child who learns to stand on her head will come away with a new sense of psychological balance and a more positive feeling about herself. Hey! She can stand on both ends! She'll also instinctively know something more about keeping her cool in a tense situation. One day, later in life when she's called on to make her first big presentation in a meeting, she may think, "Piece of cake. It can't be as hard or tricky as learning to stand on my head, and Mom taught me to do that when I was five."

62. How to Get Ketchup out of a New Bottle

If computers are so smart, why don't they tell us how to get ketchup out of a new bottle?

—Cool Mom query

You and your child go to your favorite diner for lunch. As soon as you're seated, you notice that all the tables within arm's reach are sporting new bottles of ketchup. These aren't plastic squeeze bottles. They're glass. This means your child will soon have to confront every parent's most dreaded public debut: getting the ketchup out of the glass bottle for the first time. It's here a child can get red globs all over the table and all over his shirt.

But you're not the least bit worried. That's because you know exactly how to coach your child to get ketchup out of a bottle while playing to a full house. The secret is as simple as pointing your finger.

In fact, that's what you teach your child to do: point his finger. Have him pick up the ketchup bottle and hold it horizontally above his plate. Then have him grasp the bottle between his thumb and middle finger. His forefinger should lie along the top of the bottle, pointed toward the cap. Now have him swivel his wrist downward, with a quick flicking motion, so the bottle and his forefinger suddenly point at the plate. When she brings the bottle to a sudden stop, she'll see something amazing. Coming down the neck of the bottle will be a small river of ketchup.

By flicking his wrist suddenly down, he sped up the ketchup. But when the bottle abruptly stopped moving, the ketchup continued flowing down the neck.

And voila! Your kid has just solved an age-old problem Isaac Newton couldn't solve. We're sure that even Einstein, when he tried to start a new bottle, got ketchup on his shirt.

COOL MOM FACTS

Ketchup, or catsup, is derived from the Chinese word *ke tsiap,* a brine of pickled fish or shellfish. The spiced sauce was brought to England where it appeared in print in 1690 as "catsup" and in 1711 as "ketchup," which may be the source of the controversy over the correct way to spell it. New Englanders added tomatoes to ketchup in the late 1700s. A tablespoon of ketchup has sixteen calories and no fat. Four tablespoons of ketchup are the nutritional equivalent of an entire ripe medium tomato.

63. How to Whistle with an Acorn

Feeling blue? Don't despair. Give a little whistle!

—Cool Mom advice

Whether it's made by a tea kettle, a steam engine, or the wind in the willows, whistling is one of the happiest sounds on Earth. Whenever a kid feels down in the dumps, a whistle can brighten her day.

Happily, you know a new way to whistle, and you're willing to teach it to your child—for free. You know how to whistle with an acorn. Your child just needs to create a triangular hole through which to blow.

First, show your child how to remove the cap from the acorn and hold it open side up, like a cup ready to hold water. Second, show her how to cover the opening with her thumbs (Fig. 1). Have her roll her thumbs toward each other, pressing them tightly together. The acorn cap should be completely covered except for a relatively large, triangular hole between the ends of her thumbs (as shown). Have her check to be sure she has no air leaks between her thumbs and the rim of the cap. Now have her place her lower lip near her thumb knuckles and blow gently but firmly into the acorn cap through the triangular hole.

At first the whistle may not come out. Encourage her to try blowing softer, then harder. Have her shift the angle at which she blows into the cap. At last, a sharp, shrill whistle will pierce the air. *Shreeeee!!!* Soon she'll be able to make an acorn whistle as easily as she can tap her toes.

As your child learns to force a whistle from an old acorn, she's also learning how to persist, be patient, and develop a sensitive touch to solve problems. Her renewed good cheer, in turn, will boost her confidence in her ability to rise above her problems. Life is always worthwhile to the person who can laugh, love, and whistle.

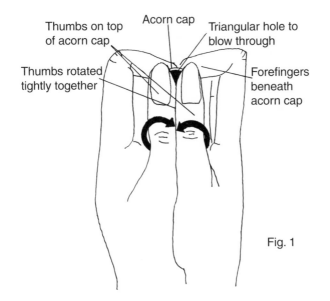

Thumbs on top of acorn cap

Acorn cap

Triangular hole to blow through

Thumbs rotated tightly together

Forefingers beneath acorn cap

Fig. 1

COOL MOM TIP

How to Eat an Acorn

Native Americans didn't make musical instruments out of acorns, but they did make surprisingly healthy food. Acorns contain 18 percent fat, 6 percent protein, and 68 percent carbohydrate (compared to corn and wheat, which are about 2 percent fat, 10 percent protein, and 75 percent carbohydrate). Acorns are also good sources of vitamins A and C and taste a bit like chestnuts.

Yet when a kid bites into an acorn, yuck! It tastes bitter. That's because acorns often contain tannins. If your child longs to sample an acorn, she can get rid of the tannins (and the bitterness). How? Shell the nuts and boil them in successive pots of water until the water no longer turns brown like tea. Then roast the acorns in a slow oven (225 degrees) for about 20 minutes. Once the nuts are crunchy and ready to eat, she can even use them in recipes. Anyone for chocolate-chip-acorn cookies?

64. How to Tell a Bug from a Beetle

God must love beetles. He made so many of them.

—Cool Mom saying

Your child has become enchanted lately by ladybugs. He wants to know everything about them. But when he goes to the library and looks up "bugs," he finds nothing about ladybugs. He's stumped. What's going on?

Well, of course, you know your young explorer's problem. A ladybug is not really a bug at all. It's a beetle. *Huh?* your kid wonders. *Bug? Beetle? What's the difference?* A beetle, you explain, always has a straight line down the middle of its back. This line marks the place where the beetle's two leathery wings meet (Fig. 1). In contrast, a bug's back usually has several distinct sections. Another name for a ladybug is a ladybird beetle. A lightning bug or firefly is also really a beetle.

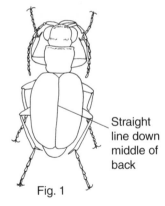

Straight line down middle of back

Fig. 1

Your young explorer can also tell a bug from a beetle by looking at the critter's mouthparts. Bugs

155

have mouthparts shaped like sharp beaks. When a bug finds a leaf or another bug to dine on, he stabs it with his "beak," then sucks out the juices through a long tube, much as if he's using a straw.

By learning to tell a bug from a beetle, your child will gain a better understanding of nature and more confidence in his own observations. And as he heads back to the library to renew his search for information about ladybird beetles, he'll know how important it is to observe small details closely. Big differences are often found in small places.

COOL MOM FACTS

- Beetles make up the largest group of living creatures on earth. So far, scientists have found more than 290,000 species.

- Bees hum, flies buzz, and grasshoppers chirp and pitter, but beetles drone.

- A grasshopper isn't a bug or a beetle: It's a hopper.

- The notion that some beetles are blind is wrong. All beetles can see. But one type, the dorbeetle or hedgechafer, flies so fast it will sometimes bump into people, so it acts blind.

- A bookworm, which likes to bore through books, is actually the larvae of some beetles (particularly the drugstore, deathwatch, and spider beetles). So if someone says you're a "bookworm," they're calling you a beetle.

65. How to Tell if a Shoe Fits

Base your taste in shoes on what doesn't pinch, slip, or gap.
—Cool Mom motto

Some children find a shiny new pair of shoes more fun than a cloud of pink cotton candy. From Dorothy's enchanted red shoes in *The Wizard of Oz* to Cinderella's midnight-magic glass slippers, new shoes promise new adventures. Maybe that's why children seldom think about choosing a shoe that fits well. When buying new shoes, they look only at the color and the style. If it's the latest fad, that's the pair they want.

But you know if a shoe fits poorly, the kid won't wear it. The wrong-sized shoe can wear blisters, cause sore toes, and even damage the growth of her foot. Years later, as many as nine in ten women still buy shoes too small for their feet and often suffer foot troubles as a result.

So now, while her foot is still growing, teach your child how to buy a shoe that fits. The secret is easy and simple: Use the thumb-width test. The shoe should be long enough to allow one thumb's width between the end of the shoe and her longest toe (Fig. 1) A shoe any longer than this may slip up and down on her heel and wear blisters. A shoe any shorter may pinch and will allow so little growing room that she may need new shoes in two months.

Before she tries on any shoes, your child should have both

her feet measured. On some kids, one foot can be as much as a size or more larger than the other. Generally, the dominant foot (the right foot if she's right-handed) will be larger. But not always. Once she finds a shoe she likes and it passes the thumb-width test, make sure she walks around on it to see how it feels. The shoe should fit the sides of her foot without gapping, and it shouldn't slip on the heel. Leather shoes can be a teensy snug on the sides (leather will stretch). But they shouldn't pinch so tightly they hurt. For most kids, especially those with skinny feet, shoes that buckle or lace up work better than slip-ons.

As your child learns how to buy a shoe that fits, she's also learning that her body's comfort matters more than how trendy a certain style or color might look. And later in life, she'll be more likely to insist that fashion fit *her* needs rather than the other way around.

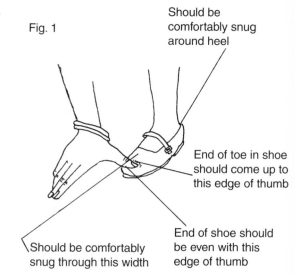

Fig. 1

Should be comfortably snug around heel

End of toe in shoe should come up to this edge of thumb

Should be comfortably snug through this width

End of shoe should be even with this edge of thumb

66. How to Kick a Soccer Ball

To want in one's head to do a thing for it's own sake; to enjoy doing it; to concentrate all one's energies upon it—that is not only the surest guarantee of success, it is also being true to oneself.

—Amelia Earhart, Cool Mom of aviation

Your kid hopes to make the soccer team this year. All his friends will be on the team. He thinks soccer sounds like a blast. Trouble is, he's never even kicked a soccer ball. What if he tries out and just looks like a geek?

But you know hoping to do something well is the first step toward doing it. Plus you know a secret about the soccer kick. It's done with the *instep* (not the toe) of the foot. Using his instep will help him control the distance, direction, and height the ball travels.

To kick correctly, your child should run to the ball and plant his non-kicking foot beside it (Fig. 1). He should then kick the ball with the instep of his kicking foot. Have him keep his kicking foot very close to the ground. He should also make sure he swings his leg *through* his kick. Many kids think once they've touched the ball with their foot, they've kicked it. They stop short and fail to follow through. This throws them off-balance. They kick poorly. Also, have him make sure he always keeps his eye on the ball.

What if the ball is rolling toward him (not just resting on the ground)? The basic skills are the same. The only difference lies in how he plants his non-kicking foot. As the ball rolls toward him, he needs to judge how fast it's rolling. Then he should plant his non-kicking foot far enough ahead of the ball so that by the time his kicking foot connects, the ball will be right beside his planted foot.

Remind him it's harder to kick well with his left leg if he's right-handed and vice versa. So he should practice a lot with his non-dominant or "off" leg. While executing the kick, he should also keep his head steady (not angled or bobbing up and down). Anytime he moves his head, the ball will appear to jump. This will make the ball harder to kick accurately.

As your child works at perfecting his kick, he's increasing his odds of making the team and looking cool in front of his friends. At the same time, he's learning that *hope* is an active verb. Almost nothing in life comes naturally to any of us. But hope activated by hard work will help him succeed at whatever he sets out to do.

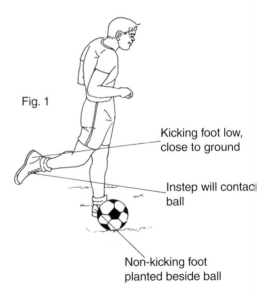

Fig. 1

Kicking foot low, close to ground

Instep will contact ball

Non-kicking foot planted beside ball

67. How to Weigh a Cloud

I dare say you haven't had much practice [at believing impossible things]. . . . Why, sometimes I've believed as many as six impossible things before breakfast.

—White Queen, Cool Mom of nonsense in
Lewis Carroll's *Through the Looking Glass*

To kids, clouds are far away and elusive. Weighing one seems rather . . . well . . . impossible. How would you get one on a scale? Even if you could, a cloud would probably weigh so little the scale wouldn't budge. Of course, you know it is possible to weigh a cloud—if you know a secret. But get ready for some loud gee-whizzes from your kid. A cloud weighs a lot more than most people think.

Here's the secret: You need to know the amount of water vapor in a cloud and how much it weighs. On a clear day, a fluffy, fair-weather cumulus cloud (non-raining) contains about ten drops of water for every clump of cloud matter the size of an average refrigerator. That's .38 grams of water per cubic yard.

Now that you know this, your child needs to guesstimate the size of the cloud to figure out how much it weighs. For example, if you live in a city, eight city blocks is roughly one mile. So if your child sees a cloud about four blocks long, then it's half a mile across.

No cloud is a cube. But for a simple calculation, let's say

this one is one-half-mile high, one-half-mile long, and one-half-mile wide. Doing the math with 880 yards to the half-mile, have your child multiply to get the volume of the cloud. In this case 880 times 880 times 880 (length times width times height) equals 681,472,000 cubic yards in our cloud. At .38 grams of water per cubic yard, it weighs in at 285 tons! That's about as much as forty large bull African elephants.

The following table shows how a fair weather cloud varies in weight according to its size.

Size of Cloud	Volume in Yds^3	Weight in Tons
1 mile^3	5,451,776,000	2283.00
1/2 mile^3	681,472,000	285.00
1/4 mile^3	85,184,000	36.00
1/8 mile^3	10,648,000	4.46

On the other hand, a gigantic rain cloud can have a volume of 2 quadrillion cubic yards and can weigh more than 28 million tons—almost ten times the weight of all the African elephants in the world. Now it so happens that rain clouds form very near the earth, under 6,500 feet. So the next time your child reads a story that says the rain clouds were low and heavy, the writer wasn't kidding. They are very, very low and very, very, very, very heavy.

While your child is sorting this all out, she's also learning about deductive reasoning. Later in life while others throw up their hands in despair over a problem that seems impossible, she'll be looking for a mathematical way to solve it. You can learn a lot by weighing a cloud.

68. How to Field a Bunt with One Hand

The smart player knows the rules. But the smarter player also knows the exceptions.

—Cool Mom saying

Your kid's in Little League. He already knows a lot about baseball. He knows, for example, that he should always field a ball with two hands. There will come moments, however—such as when he's playing third and a weak grounder or bunted ball comes directly at him—that he needs to break that rule. He needs to field the ball with one hand and whip a throw across his body to first base. He has no other choice, except to "eat" the ball (baseball lingo for looking like a dork).

As baseballs are not part of your child's daily diet and he's definitely no dork, you decide to teach him how to field a baseball with one hand. The secret is this: He should never reach out for the ball. If he does, he'll very likely hit the ball with his fingertips and knock it away. The runner will then run easily to first or even to second.

Instead, teach him to charge toward home plate, stop beside the rolling ball, drop his hand (palm up) on the ground, then wait long enough for the ball to roll into his hand. Once he has a good grip on the ball, he can take one step forward, swing his arm across his chest, and throw to first. This flashy play will take an extra few seconds at first. But with practice, he'll soon be scooping up grounders and then rocketing bullets to first base.

To help your child practice this play, have him stand about halfway between home and third base. Then as you stand at home plate, roll the ball easily toward him on the ground. He should practice charging in, stopping, dropping his hand to the ground, and allowing the ball to roll into his hand. Then he should make the throw to first.

Learning to field a ground ball with one hand will build his confidence, and he'll feel great when making this play in a game. But he'll also learn another rule for success: Always play within the rules of the game—but don't forget to add your own flashy touches.

COOL MOM TIP

How to Throw Sidearm

Any child who plays the infield should learn to throw sidearm. This is especially true if he plays third base, short-stop, or second base. The secret to throwing sidearm is this: Never lift your hand above your shoulder. Just whip the ball across your body. With this throw, your kid won't have to straighten up to complete the play. This saves time. But fore-warn your child that sidearm throws tend to sail into Never-Never Land. He needs to practice throwing sidearm a lot before trying it in a game.

69. How to Do a Backbend

Getting fit is a political act—you are taking charge of your life.
— Jane Fonda, Cool Mom of work-out tapes

Kids are so elastic and springy, they're all a bit like Gumby. They love twisting their bodies into pretzel-like shapes, as stiffer-jointed adults marvel, "My word, however did you tie yourself into such a knot?" Yet when most kids try to do a backbend, they do it all wrong. They lie with their backs flat on the floor and push up stiffly with their arms. Then they scuttle across the ground on all fours like an upside-down crab.

But your child can do a backbend with the flexibility of an Olympic gymnast. That's because you've taught her the secret. Starting from a standing position, she needs to bend over backwards at the waist until she can see the floor over her head. When she sees the floor, she'll know she's in the right position to complete the backbend correctly. Here are the steps:

1. Have your kid stand with her hands on her hips and her feet apart. Her feet should be splayed wide enough to lower her body a few inches closer to the floor, but not so far apart she loses her balance.

2. With her hands still on her hips, have her bend back at the waist—farther, farther, farther—there! Suddenly, she'll see the floor over her head behind her.

3. Once she sees the floor, she should swing her arms over her head, arch her back even further, and drop backwards, breaking her fall with her hands. This last step should be done in one fluid motion. If she's afraid to fall backwards (as many kids are), place your hands firmly under the arch of her back. Tell her you'll hold her as she drops so she won't fall and get hurt. Soon she'll be stretching herself into a backbend every chance she gets.

As your child develops more confidence in her supple body, she may also develop a more supple sense of self-esteem. One day she may decide that being flexible can be an asset at whatever she sets out to do. It's those able to stretch themselves to embrace new ideas who most easily bounce back when the going gets tough.

70. How to Answer "What's the Meaning of Life?"

Some people go through life trying to find out what the world holds for them only to find out too late that it's what they bring to the world that really counts.

—Anne, Cool Mom of Green Gables

Since you had so many answers ready for your child when he was small, he will one day grow older and ask you the profoundest of questions: "Mom, what's the meaning of life?" And, of course, you've been waiting for this one for years. You have the answer right on the tip of your tongue.

"That," you say, "is not the question you ask of life. It is the question that life asks of you—and you must answer it with your actions." You can tell your kid that Victor E. Frankl, a Viennese psychiatrist, spent his entire life studying this question, and that's basically what he concluded. We're each responsible for the meanings of our own existence.

Many people try to dodge this responsibility by pretending life has no meaning. They want easy answers. When the answers get tough, they give up and stop trying. Then they feel hopeless, lost, and depressed. They say, "I couldn't do any better." "That's the way I was brought up." "My life never went right because I got all the tough breaks." They look outside themselves for excuses to fail. But people who find hope and meaning rise above their problems.

During World War II, Dr. Frankl was a prisoner in Nazi concentration camps where he found that even in the most wretched of conditions life still has a meaning. In his classic book *Man's Search for Meaning* (which your child may want to read), Dr. Frankl wrote: "We who lived in concentration camps can remember the men who walked through the huts comforting others, giving away their last piece of bread. They may have been few in number, but they offer sufficient proof that everything can be taken from a man but one thing: the last of the human freedoms—to choose one's attitude in any given set of circumstances, to choose one's own way." Dr. Frankl also observed, "What [man] becomes—within the limits of environment and endowment—is what he has made out of himself." After being released from the camps, Dr. Frankl remarried, had a family, wrote twenty-seven books about finding meaning in life, and lived to age ninety-three.

You can tell your child that all great religions have offered meaningful answers to life's questions, and these answers inevitably involve some form of love and responsible service to others.

Kids often plead, "Tell me the meaning of life [so I won't have to work]." But, of course, you know that the meaning of life is that you have to work. No one else can tell your child the meaning of his life. But he's here for something only he can do, and it is vitally important that he do it.

Next question?

71. How to Wiggle Your Ears

Happiness is not a possession to be prized, it is a quality of thought, a state of mind.

—Daphne du Maurier, Cool Mom of *Rebecca*

Every kid regularly needs to let her silly, nutty side out to play, and it's good to be happy-go-lucky. Unfortunately, good-natured silliness can degenerate into rowdy behavior that irritates onlookers. This need not happen. There is a way for your child to be silly, whenever she feels the urge, that is surprisingly pleasant and even interesting to the quiet ones around her. Teach her the Cool Mom skill of wiggling her ears.

Many kids can't wiggle their ears. They don't know the right muscles to move. But, of course, you know those muscles. They're the ones just in front of, above, and behind the ear (Fig. 1). Have your child envision these ear-wiggling muscles as a sort of helmet around each ear. For the ears to wiggle, these muscles have to be flexed. How? Have her contract her scalp. If she has natural ear-wiggling talents, she may be able to flap her ears in the breeze on the first try.

What if she can't do it? Then give her a little help. Have her cup her ears with her hands. Her thumbs should be on her earlobes, her fingertips lightly touching the edges of her ears. Now have her contract her scalp again until she feels her ears move. That's when she'll know she's located the correct muscles.

As your kid giggles with delight over her newfound "talent," she'll also be learning that the ability to laugh at oneself is the essence of a good sense of humor, which brings joy and happiness to everyone around her. As the Buddhists say, "Only happy people can make a happy world." Sometimes nonsense makes good sense.

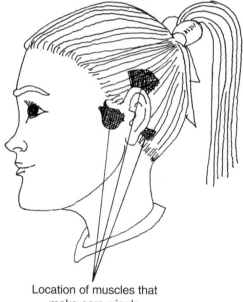

Location of muscles that
make ears wiggle

Cool Mom Song

A song to sing While Wiggling One's Ears (sing to the tune of "Turkey in the Straw"

Do your ears hang low?
Do they wobble to and fro?
Can you tie them in a knot?
Can you tie them in a bow?
Can you throw them o'er your shoulder
Like a Continental Soldier?
Do your ears hang low?

Do your ears hang wide?
Do they flap from side to side?
Do they wave in the breeze?
From the slightest little sneeze?
Can you soar above the nation
With a sense of elevation?
Do your ears hang wide?

Do your ears hang high?
Do they reach up to the sky?
Do they wrinkle when they're wet?
Do they straighten when they're dry?
Can you wave them at your neighbor
With an element of flavor?
Do your ears hang high?

Do your ears fall off?
When you give a great big cough
Do they lie there on the ground
Or bounce up at every sound?
Can you stick them in your pocket
Just like Davy Crocket?
Do your ears fall off?

72. How to Find the Oldest Thing You'll Ever See

Eternity is not something that begins after you are dead. It is going on all the time. We are in it now.

— Charlotte Perkins Gilman, Cool Mom poet, lecturer, and social critic

Kids love knowing the records for the biggest, the fastest, the strongest . . . So show your kid the oldest thing she'll ever see. She only has to step outside on any warm summer night. When she looks up at the sky almost directly overhead, she'll see Arcturus. Older than the Earth, older even than the sun, this star was formed about 10 billion years ago. It's the oldest thing she'll ever see with her naked eye.

One of the first stars named by the ancients and the only star mentioned by name in the Bible, Arcturus is easy to find. Simply find the Big Dipper. Then follow along the arc of the Big Dipper's handle and make an arc to Arcturus. Tell your child to follow the arc with her eye across the night sky until she sees a dazzlingly bright star with a slightly orange tinge. That's Arcturus, the fourth brightest star in the sky. If it were set right beside our sun, Arcturus would shine 180 times brighter. It is located in a constellation called Bootes, which is shaped like a kite. As your child will see, Arcturus is located at the point of the kite where the tail would be attached.

You can tell your child that Arcturus is 36.7 light years away. A light year is the distance light travels through space in one year. Since light speeds through black space at the colossal rate of 186,000 miles per second, this means light travels a huge distance in one year—about 5,865,696,000,000 miles. That's nearly six trillion miles. As your child ponders this gee-whiz fact, you can go on to explain that the light striking her eyes tonight left Arcturus more than 36 years ago. This means the light she's seeing now traveled 215,271,043,200,000 miles—or more than 215 trillion miles—to arrive here tonight.

In these days of rapid change, there's something comforting about meeting a star that's so old. And the next time your child pipes up from the backseat of the car, "Are we there yet?" you can gently remind her of the light from Arcturus, and perhaps she'll tone down her impatience. At least she doesn't have to ride another 215 trillion miles.

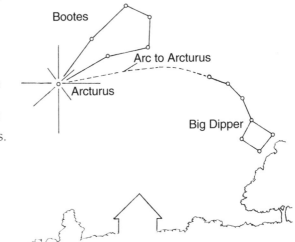

73. How to Use a Wrench

Enthusiasm is good. But too much enthusiasm coupled with too little knowledge can really wreck a bolt.

—Cool Mom observation

Nothing makes a little kid feel more like a big kid than using a real tool. But the kid who decides to be Mr. Goodwrench with no help is headed for trouble. Determined to fix his bike, he'll grab the biggest, shiniest wrench he can find and start fanatically twisting. Soon he's jimmied up the bolt and scraped his knuckles. Meanwhile, his bike still needs to be repaired—at a shop.

So before your child gets himself into this jam, teach him how to use a wrench. Although wrenches come in many different styles, the most versatile type for light jobs is the adjustable crescent-type wrench. If he has only one wrench, it should be this one. With just one adjustable wrench, your kid can fix his bike, his skateboard, his swing set, his scooter, and a whole bunch of other stuff.

Just one adjustable wrench can take the place of sixteen or more non-adjustable (or fixed) wrenches. A fixed wrench is like a pair of expensive slacks: It fits only one size. An adjustable wrench is more like a pair of polyester pants with a stretchy waist: It can expand or contract to fit many sizes.

How does this snazzy wrench work? Easy. One side (or jaw)

of the wrench stays solidly in one place, the other side moves (Fig. 1). By turning the thumbscrew adjustment (Fig. 1), your kid can adjust the wrench to fit many different-sized nuts.

When he uses the wrench, your child should carefully tighten the jaws so they fit the nut snugly. The nut should be flat against the adjustable jaw (as shown). He should also always pull the wrench handle toward him rather than pushing it away. If he pushes the handle away from his body, the wrench can slip off the nut. His hand could slip with it, and his knuckles could get scraped. If you want to impress him with this idea, you can tell him this wrench was nicknamed "the knuckle buster" by sloppy people who didn't know how to use it.

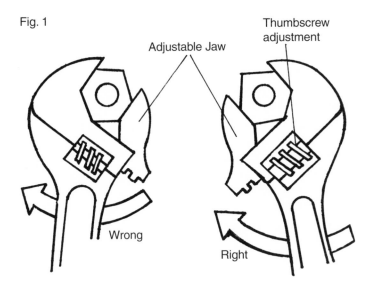

Fig. 1

Thumbscrew adjustment

Adjustable Jaw

Wrong

Right

By methodically paying attention to small details, your child will learn how to do the job right, and his confidence will blossom. Knowing how to do little jobs well always makes us feel bigger.

COOL MOM TIP

What Size Wrench Should You Buy?

Although each wrench can fit many different-sized nuts, adjustable crescent-type wrenches do come in many sizes. The size of an adjustable wrench is measured by the length of its handle. A wrench with a six-inch handle is called a "six-inch wrench." One with a twelve-inch handle is a "twelve-inch wrench," and so on. Tell your kid that even though the wrench can be adjusted, he should still try to match the size of his wrench to the size of his bolt. If he tries to loosen a tiny nut with a giant wrench, he can sheer that bolt right off and bloody his knuckles. A six-inch adjustable wrench is probably best for most jobs he'll tackle.

---

74. How to Be Bold at the Plate

Courage is rarely reckless or foolish . . . courage usually involves a highly realistic estimate of the odds that must be faced.
—Margaret Truman Daniel, author, editor, and Cool Mom of four

Standing at home plate as a stranger whizzes hard, leather-covered baseballs past your head can be scary. If a child sees another batter get hit by a pitch, that only confirms his worst fears. Telling your kid the pitcher's not trying to hit him probably won't be reassuring. Soon he may flinch at every pitch. That's a bad habit to learn.

Fortunately, you know a surefire way to help your child beat his fear of getting hit by a pitch. It will also make him hit better. He just needs to learn the strike zone.

Once he knows the strike zone, he'll be bolder. He'll see the ball is usually headed not toward him, but some distance away from him—toward the strike zone. On those rare occasions when an aggressive pitcher gives the batter a little "chin music" to keep him from crowding the plate, your child will also know enough to get out of the way.

One of the best ways to teach your child how to judge the strike zone is to deck him out in catcher's equipment: mask, chest pad, shin guards, mitt, the whole works. Then have him stand at the plate with the bat on his shoulder as you toss tennis balls past him. Tell him not to swing at any of these pitches. When a pitch looks in or out of the strike zone, you just want him to call out "strike" or "ball." Any ball he thinks might be about to hit him he can snag with the catcher's mitt.

Now have him remove one piece of catching equipment at a time as he feels more and more secure. Finally, when he's no longer wearing any catcher's equipment, stand him in front of a garage door and throw tennis balls past him. Mark the strike zone behind him on the garage door. As he calls the pitches, you can see if he's right or wrong. After he gets to the point where he can call a large percentage of the pitches correctly, you can switch to a baseball.

Eventually, your child can again start swinging the bat. But now that he trusts his own judgment and knows where those pitches are headed, he'll swing with authority. He'll improve his batting average immensely. At the same time, he'll have learned that acquiring the habit of prudent action is a good way to get rid of fear.

75. How to Get a Bird to Talk

I am sure there is magic in everything, only we have not sense enough to get hold of it and make it do things for us.

—Frances Hodgson Burnett,
Cool Mom of *The Secret Garden*

Many classic children's stories involve animals that can talk. Why? Because an animal that truly speaks suggests Magic is at work in the world. When a bird (like a budgie) talks, a child wonders, *Could this be Magic?* Every time the bird says something, he's amazed and delighted.

But what's the secret to getting a bird to talk? Your child has to pick out the right bird. Like people, birds have their own personalities. Some outgoing, chatty types pick up words immediately. Others are shy—and eternally silent. To get a bird to talk, your child needs to pick out one that *will* talk.

Of the large birds, the macaws and parrots (particularly the African grey) are the chattiest. Of the small birds, the best talker is the parakeet, or budgie. Female birds tend to talk less than males. Old birds are harder to train than young ones. It's also better to buy just one bird (not a pair). A single bird will more likely bond with your child and will therefore want to chat.

There are a few easy tests your child can give a pet-shop bird to see how likely it will be to talk once you get it home.

Have your child watch all the birds in the cage. Is one shy

and withdrawn while another seems lively and perky? Your child should be looking for a male bird who seems alert and interested in his surroundings.

Once she's chosen a bird she likes, have her try talking to it and see how it responds to her voice. If the bird squawks in fear or shies away as she approaches the cage, that's a sign it won't talk easily. She should try another bird. The bird she wants is the one that looks at her curiously and babbles happily. Have your child watch the birds in the cage for fifteen minutes or so to make sure she's got the one that looks like the best talker.

Once home, your child should give the bird some time to adjust to its new surroundings. Then have her interact a lot with the bird. She should softly and gently repeat the words she hopes it will say. Have her keep it short and simple. Good beginning phrases are "Hi (child's name)" and "How are you?" Remind her the bird will repeat the words it hears most often. So if the bird's name is Dinky and she often says, "Hi, Dinky," the bird will learn that phrase.

Day by day, as your child teaches her bird to talk, she's acquiring a life-long habit that will serve her well: a willingness to wait and listen until the other guy has his say.

76. How to Take a Snapshot

A good snapshot stops a moment from running away.
          —Eudora Welty, a Cool Mom of American literature

To a child, a camera is an object of wonder. He's seen you take pictures of Aunt Louise and Uncle Cy. He's half-convinced you're not merely rolling the film forward, pointing the camera, and clicking the shutter. You must be performing a miracle. Could he possibly get the same results?

Well, no. If your pictures are good, he probably can't. If he takes the camera and just shoots whatever catches his eye, the cat will resemble a long black bean on the horizon, and Aunt Mary's head will be sprouting a flag pole.

The secret when taking a snapshot is to compose the picture. Composing means thinking about his picture ahead of time to show the subjects off to their best advantage. Nothing in the background should distract from the subjects or make them look silly. Nothing in the foreground should suddenly dash into the picture at the last second. For example, he doesn't want a cat leaping out after the canary he's photographing and ruining everything. So here are some basics he should think about:

- Have your child focus on getting his subject in the front and center. He should get as close as possible to his subject and try to fill the whole frame.
- Most kids tend to stand back too far from the action. So encourage your child to move in. Even when he thinks he's close enough to shoot, have him move another step closer.
- Your child can add interest to his photo by getting up (or down) to his subject's eye level. If he's photographing the dog, have him lie on the floor. At Thanksgiving dinner, have him crouch down to table-top height. Once again, have him notice the background, so Grandfather's cup of eggnog isn't sprouting a vase of roses or his sister doesn't have a cuckoo suddenly popping out of her ear.
- Of course, you'll want to check the film to make sure it's correctly loaded. And, inside or even outside (on a dark day), he'll want to use a flash.

As your child learns to take a great snapshot, he's learning how to look more closely at small details. At the same time, he'll have captured a precious moment forever. Everything on this earth changes. But as Anne Morrow Lindbergh, a Cool Mom of five, once declared, the beauty of a photograph is that "when people change, old pictures of them don't change along with them."

77. How to Watch Things That Live in Yucky Water

Curiosity, the seed of all genius, grows stronger when it's gratified. Never let anyone stunt your creative curiosity.

—Cool Mom saying

Any child who sees a trout swimming in a clear mountain brook or a crab skittering in a tidal pool begins to wonder: What mysterious life forms lurk beneath the water's surface in scummy ponds and mud puddles? Your child's curiosity is piqued. But she obviously can't put her face down into that murky water to find out.

So how can your kid explore the world's black lagoons without endangering her health? Simple. Use an "underwater viewer." It's cheap and easy to make. Yet it will protect your child from any slime-borne disease or other nasty creature that might lurk in the darkness below.

An underwater viewer works just like water goggles except your kid doesn't have to get her face wet. Here's how your child can make an underwater viewer out of an old milk carton, a large rubber band, and some clear plastic wrap.

Have her take a half-gallon cardboard milk carton and cut off both ends. Then have her stretch plastic wrap over the bottom of the carton, securing the wrap with a rubber band (Fig. 1).

Now you and your child can take turns putting the viewer into the yucky water and exploring life beneath the pond's surface. If you place the viewer gently in the water and hold it there a few minutes, turtles, fish, and other pond life may not even know you're watching.

By teaching your child to make an underwater viewer, you're encouraging her to improvise to satisfy her curiosity. Later in life, she'll be one of those imaginative people who aren't easily stumped by unusual questions. She'll just look for an unusual way to find the right answers.

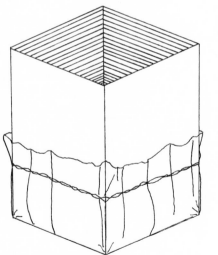

Fig. 1

78. How to Build a Tire Swing

How we spend our days is, of course, how we spend our lives.
        —Annie Dillard, Cool Mom of *The Pilgrim of Tinker Creek*

There's nothing quite as happy as a tire swing. As a kid sucks a popsicle and gently floats through the air, his thoughts can be a million miles away. *What's it like right now on Jupiter? Do spiders have toes? Why don't white ducks fly?* In this high-tech age of seventy-mile-per-hour freeways, gigahertz computers, and fast food, daydreaming often gets lost in the shuffle. So let your kid taste what it *really* means to be laid-back and cool. Build him a tire swing.

First you need a backyard tree with one good, strong limb sprouting directly out from the trunk ten to twenty feet in the air. Once you've got that, here's the secret to making a tire swing that lasts. Between the rope and the limb over which you hang the rope, you need to place a cut-out piece of rubber (Fig. 1). This rubber will keep the back and forth motion of the swing from eating into the limb, so it won't break.

Now, to get started, you'll need:

Cut out piece of tire to go over limb of tree

Fig. 1

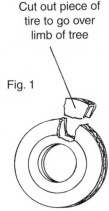

- Two old tires: one for the swing, the second for the cut-out piece of rubber. Forget steel-belted radials. They're too hard to cut. The sharp cords can also pierce the rubber and hurt a kid.
- Rope for hanging the tire.
- Two pieces of board, one two-by-two-by-three or four inches (depending on the size of the tire), the other two-by-four-by-eight inches.
- Nails, 8- to 10-penny size.
- A sharp knife (like a tar-paper knife) that will cut rubber tires.

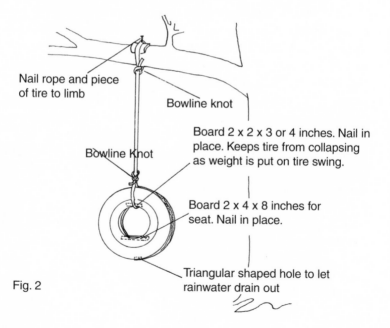

Nail rope and piece of tire to limb

Bowline knot

Bowline Knot

Board 2 x 2 x 3 or 4 inches. Nail in place. Keeps tire from collapsing as weight is put on tire swing.

Board 2 x 4 x 8 inches for seat. Nail in place.

Triangular shaped hole to let rainwater drain out

Fig. 2

1. From the second old tire (the one you're *not* using for the swing), cut a piece of rubber about eight or ten inches long (Fig. 1).

2. Place the shorter piece of board on the inside and at the top of the tire you're using for the swing (Fig. 2). Nail it in place.

3. Cut a small triangular hole dead-center in the bottom of the swing, to provide a run-out for rainwater.

4. Place the longer piece of board in the tire at the bottom to make a seat. Nail it in place.

5. Hang the rope over the limb of the tree. Protect the tree limb with the piece of rubber you cut in Step 1. Nail the rubber to the limb. This will not hurt the limb.

6. Attach the rope to the tire, as shown, and *voila!* You're done.

For less than ten bucks, you've built a tire swing on which your kid can idle away many a lazy summer day. In this fast-paced, high-tech world, you've given him a piece of a rare and precious gift: a happy, unhurried childhood.

COOL MOM TIP

How to Tie a Bowline

The bowline is one of the easiest of all knots to tie. Yet it won't lip or jam. Here's how to tie one.

79. How to Tell a Tree's Age (Without Cutting it Down)

Surely it is cruel to cut down a very fine tree! Each dull, dead thud of the axe hurts the little green fairy that lives inside its heart.
—Beatrix Potter, Cool Mom of *Peter Rabbit*

Maybe it's because they've been around for so few years, but children are fascinated with age. How old is that house? How old is a rock? How old is that tree? In the case of the house, you can usually tell by the architectural style approximately when it was built. Rocks require a lot of scientific investigation. But in the case of that tree, you can usually tell how old it is at a glance.

That's because you know that most trees add about an inch to their circumference every year. So just by measuring (or estimating) how big around a tree is, in inches, you can often tell approximately how old it is, in years. For the most accurate measurement, have your child place a string or tape measure around the tree trunk about five feet above the ground.

This rule of thumb, of course, doesn't work for some fast-growing or slow-growing trees—especially not for stunted dwarf trees (bonsai trees, for instance). It also does not work with redwood or sequoia trees. For example, the world's fattest (as opposed to tallest) tree is a giant sequoia tree named General Sherman in Sequoia National Park. At five feet above the ground, General Sherman is 36.5 feet—or 438 inches—in diameter. Yet it's estimated to be about 3,500 years old. Trees like General Sherman are dated by *dendrochronology* (the science of dating trees by their rings). But most trees are as old in years as they are big around in inches.

As your child learns to think about the age of the trees she sees, she may gain (as many do) a greater sense of stability and security. An old tree is a monument to life's ability to adapt and endure despite change. And one day, while walking along a soft trail through the forest with flecks of sunlight filtering through a canopy of leaves overhead, she may find her thoughts uplifted, just knowing how long those trees have been on the Earth. There's something soothing about an old tree.

COOL MOM FACTS

The World's Oldest Trees

- The Earth's oldest living tree is a bristlecone pine in the White Mountains of California. Known as "Methuselah," the tree is more than 4,700 years old. It was just a seedling when the pyramids were built and was already an ancient giant when Christ was born.
- A giant redwood, whatever its age, is like a giant water tank. A large redwood can release five hundred gallons of water into the air every day.

80. How to Eat Spaghetti Like an Italian

Everything you see I owe to spaghetti.
> —Sophia Loren, Cool Mom of Italian actresses

If you're a kid, spaghetti can be intimidating. Spaghetti in public can be terrifying. How do you get the stuff from the plate to your mouth? You can't stab or scoop it. It's not a finger food. You can't drink it. Confused but bold, most kids dive in anyway. And *slurp, slip, sloop.* The spaghetti winds up in their laps or on the floor, and they've got sauce stains on the tablecloth and their shirts. As they get their spaghetti cut up into bite-sized bits so they can eat it with a spoon, they feel incompetent.

But your child can lift long strands of his spaghetti in one neat bundle up to his mouth. That's because you've taught him how to eat spaghetti like an Italian. The secret is all in the twirling.

Fig. 1

First, show your child how to place his fork against the edge of his plate with the tines straddling several strands of spaghetti (Fig. 1).

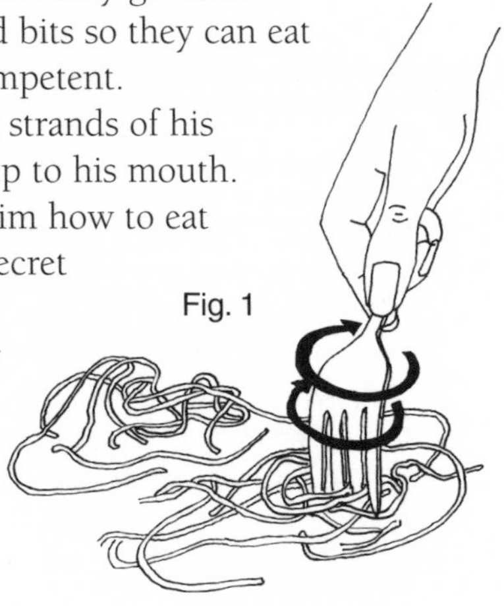

As he holds the tines against the plate, have him rotate the fork. As he spins the fork, the spaghetti will gradually become completely wrapped around the tines. Once all the ends of the spaghetti are tidily wrapped up (no loose ends), he can neatly lift the pasta to his mouth (Fig.2).

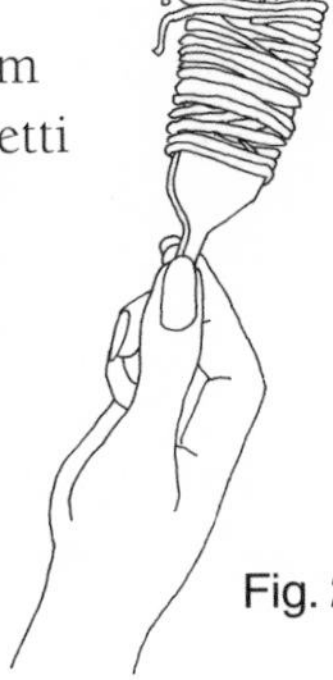

Fig. 2

At the same time your kid learns to eat his pasta with the elegance of a Roman, he's also learning another lesson. Politeness is not some mysterious talent that's inborn. It's a skill anybody can learn.

COOL MOM TIPS

- Tell your kid not to try twirling too many strands of spaghetti at once. Have him start with one to three and observe the results.

- Have him be sure to stop his last twirl as the tailing end of the spaghetti strands are going up the side of his fork. If the tail end flips over the fork, it can begin to unravel as he lifts the fork to his mouth.

- Remind him he doesn't have to eat each twirl he tries to pick up. It's sometimes best to stop twirling, let the pasta slip off the fork, and start all over again.

81. How to Tell How Fast the Wind's Blowing

Who has seen the wind? / Neither you nor I; / But when the trees bow down their heads, / The wind is passing by.
                    —Christina Rossetti, Cool Mom of English verse

Your child can't see the wind. So how can she tell anything about it? Well, that's the same question a British admiral named Sir Francis Beaufort asked back in 1805. So he developed the Beaufort Scale. With this nifty scale, anyone can judge the speed of the wind. Your child only has to observe the way smoke rises from a chimney or the way the breeze rustles the trees.

So teach your child the Beaufort Scale. It will tell her when the wind is at its best for flying her kite. It will also come in handy for the rest of her life.

Scale	Clues to Look For	What to Call It	Wind Speed
0	Air still, chimney smoke rises straight up.	calm	Less than 1 m.p.h.
1	Smoke drifts lazily in the wind.	light air	1-3 m.p.h.
2	You feel wind on your face, leaves rustle, flags stir, weather vanes turn.	light breeze	4-7 m.p.h.

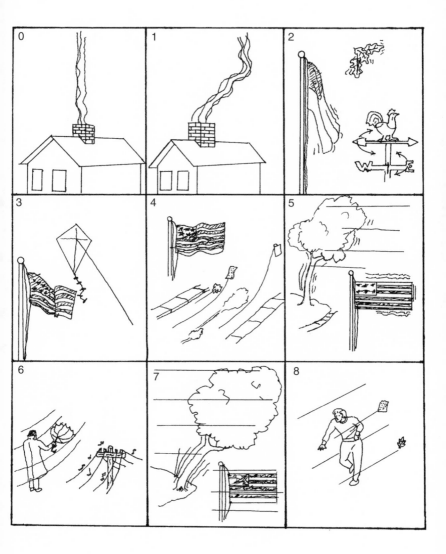

Scale	Clues to Look For	What to Call It	Wind Speed
3	Leaves and twigs move constantly, flags flutter, a good wind for kite flying.	gentle breeze	8–12 m.p.h.
4	Wind raises dust and loose papers, small branches move, flags flap	moderate breeze	13–18 m.p.h.
5	Small, leafy trees sway, flags ripple.	fresh breeze	19–24 m.p.h.
6	Large branches move, flags beat, umbrellas turn inside out, telephone wires whistle.	strong breeze	25–31 m.p.h.
7	Whole trees move, flags blow straight out.	moderate gale	32–38 m.p.h.
8	Twigs break off trees, it's hard to walk.	fresh gale	39–46 m.p.h.
9	Large branches break, TV antennas and shingles blow off, awnings rip.	strong gale	47–54 m.p.h.
10	Trees are uprooted, major damage.	storm	55–63 m.p.h.
11	Usually only in coastal areas or at sea, widespread damage.	violent storm	64–75 m.p.h.

Scale	Clues to Look For	What to Call It	Wind Speed
12	Coastal towns are leveled; major disaster.	hurricane	76+ m.p.h.

By learning to tell how fast the wind's blowing, your child is learning something important about the everyday world. And later in life, when cynics try to convince her she should never believe in anything she can't see, she'll just laugh and reply, "Oh, yeah? What about the wind?"

82. How to Pitch Better

Baseball is played on the fields of the imagination as much as on the diamond.

—Elinor Nauen, cool editor of
Diamonds Are a Girl's Best Friend

Throwing a baseball slower than any other kid on the block may sound like no big deal. But in the strange world of baseball, it can be a distinct advantage.

This is especially true if your kid already has a good fastball. If a fastball is your kid's only pitch, he'll become too predictable. The opposing batters will be onto him after a few innings. They'll start getting hits. This is an age-old problem in baseball. Even major-league pitchers need at least three different pitches to be effective. Some pitchers (like the great Catfish Hunter, who worked so effectively for the Yankees and A's in the 1980s) have four or five.

So it's time to teach your child a second pitch. Once he has a fairly good fastball, the most effective pitch you can teach him is the letup. The letup's secret? He needs to throw it as if he were pulling down a window blind. In baseball talk, when he throws a letup, he's "pulling the string."

The sneaky thing about the letup is that it's thrown with the same motion as his fastball. He appears to be throwing a fastball. That's how the batter gets fooled. In the middle of his delivery, your kid should simply change his hand motion. At the top of his motion, tell him to drop his hand straight down, as if he's pulling the string on a window blind. The batter will see his hand as traveling fast. But when your kid lets go of the ball, he'll release a lazy floater. Expecting a hot fastball, the poor batter will get tied up in knots. This usually results in lots of pop flies and easy outs.

As your child adds another pitch to his repertoire, he's also learning the advantage of versatility (which is one aspect of genius).

COOL MOM FACT

The Girl Who Struck Out Babe Ruth and Lou Gehrig

On April 2, 1931, in an exhibition game in Chattanooga, Tennessee, seventeen-year-old Jackie Mitchell—a girl—struck out two of baseball's legendary sluggers, Babe Ruth and Lou Gehrig, back to back. Jackie had only one pitch—a wicked dropping curve ball. But it was enough to blow away both Ruth ("The Sultan of Swat") and Gehrig ("The Iron Horse"). A few days later, Jackie was banned from minor-league baseball by Baseball Commissioner Kennesaw Mountain Landis, who proclaimed the sport "too strenuous for a woman." Disappointed, she played a few more years in barnstorming leagues, but eventually dropped out of baseball and went to work in her father's optometry office.

Still, Jackie Mitchell goes down in baseball history as one of the most phenomenal women ever to step on the mound. So if your daughter wants to be a pitcher, tell her she's following in the footsteps of a legend. You go, Girl!

83. How to Make a Tin-Can Telephone

Being a child at home alone in the summer is a high-risk occupation. If you call your mother at work thirteen times an hour, she can hurt you.

—Erma Bombeck, Cool Mom of family humor

The telephone may be the single most important invention since the compass. Kids love the idea they can pick up the telephone and talk at a moment's notice to anyone around the world. Unfortunately, if your kid's grandparents happen to live across the ocean, this can cost you a small fortune. A kid can also call a busy mother at work, if not thirteen times an hour, at least far too often. So help your child satisfy her communication urges without wrecking your bank account or your career. Teach her how to build a tin-can telephone. With this nifty invention, she and her friends can send messages from tree house to backyard tent to leaf house anytime they please—and it won't cost you a dime.

The secret to making a tin-can telephone work is the string. A voice is a series of vibrations. A string or small wire running between two tin cans transmits those vibrations—if it's pulled tight.

Just have your kid follow these steps:

1. Take two clean, empty tin cans. Check the cans to make sure they have no sharp edges on which someone could get cut. Cover the edges of the cans with duct tape.

2. With a large nail, hammer one hole in the bottom of each can.

3. Thread one end of a long string, piece of twine, or small wire through the hole in one can. Knot it from the inside. Now unroll the string to the desired length (even fifty to one hundred feet is fine).

4. Clip the string and thread it through the hole in the other can. Now once again, knot the string on the inside of the can. Then move the cans farther from each other, pulling the wire or string tight. Have your child talk into her can while her friend has the other can pressed to his ear. He'll be amazed to discover your child's voice comes through loud and clear.

She's just made a tin-can telephone that actually works. She and her friends can talk on it for hours without costing you a penny. They can use it all summer.

As your child learns how to make a tin-can telephone, she's also learning the power of her own ingenuity. And later in life, she'll be less likely to be one of those people who always needs to follow in the footsteps of others. She'll have acquired the habit of devising her own ingenious solutions.

84. How to Have a Snowball Fight

A snowball fight's a jolly thing / With a happy style. / Where else you gonna have a fight / While laughing all the while?

—Cool Mom poem

When they have a snowball fight, most kids just hurl snowballs helter-skelter. *Whop!* Any opponent within shooting range gets a *splat!* Such a chaotic free-for-all has a certain wild charm. But if too many icy balls hit the skies, *kersmack!* A kid could get hurt.

As the battle wages fiercely outside, are you snugly tucked away in the kitchen fixing hot chocolate? No way. You're right out in the middle of the action. That's because you know a really cool way to have a snowball fight. Use the Marquess of Queensbury Rules. This strategy offers high adventure yet keeps the battle under control.

These rules for a snowball fight were originally invented by Peter Stark and Steven M. Krauzer, who wrote a book titled *Winter Adventure*. The rules are named for the Marquess of Queensburry, a British nobleman whose ground rules transformed bare-knuckle brawling into organized boxing.

Here's how The Rules work:

First, you need enough kids for two teams, each with its

own captain. Have each team build a two-foot-high "fort" (a wall high enough to duck behind). Then have each captain assign the players on his team special duties, according to their strengths. Each team will need:

- A "dodger"—The fastest kid, one who can zig and zag out from behind the fort wall and scavenge new supplies of snow without getting plastered
- Several "riflers"—Kids with strong arms who can pop up fast, spot an enemy and hit a bull's-eye on the first try
- A "mortar"—The kid who's perfected the art of lobbing large snow cannonballs high in the air
- An "ammo maker"—A small, fast kid who can hide behind the battlements and pack fresh snowballs, passing them on to his teammates

Encourage the kids to invent their own scoring system. A grazed arm or leg might be one point. A full-bellied splat might be four points. "Rounds"— ten or twelve of them, whatever the kids decide—can last three to five minutes. On your mark, get set, go! The war is on!

As the kids learn to have a snowball fight by The Rules, they will also come to understand the importance of having a code of fair play. And after the battle, the gang will have plenty of time to retreat to the fireside, warm their toes, and swap war stories. Anyone for hot chocolate?

85. How to Lead a Horse

You can lead a horse to water if he doesn't step on your foot.
—Cool Mom saying

Whether she's horseback riding at summer camp or visiting a friend on a farm, your child might suddenly be called upon to lead a horse. It looks easy. Just pick up the rope, and the horse will intelligently follow, right? Wrong. It's a myth that horses are smart. Though usually lovable, they're big and dumb. Without meaning to, a horse can step on a kid's foot or even drag her across a meadow. The child who doesn't know how to lead a horse correctly can get seriously hurt.

So before your child ever gets around a horse, teach her the correct way to lead one. She needs to grip the rope firmly and act completely in charge. But at the same time, she needs to stay out of the horse's way and be ready to drop the rope if she needs to.

Tell her to walk to one side of the horse (left or right, it doesn't matter), using one hand to hold the lead rope firmly near the horse's head. The rest of the rope should be coiled neatly—but loosely—in her other hand (Fig. 1). She should always walk to one side of the horse so he won't step on her or run her down if he gets spooked.

The worst mistake your child can make when leading a horse is to tie the rope around her waist or wrap it tightly

Fig. 1

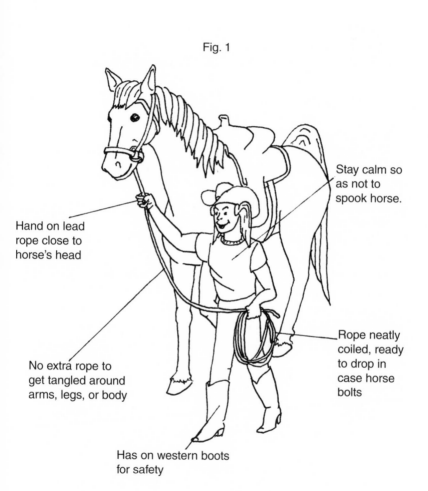

Stay calm so as not to spook horse.

Hand on lead rope close to horse's head

No extra rope to get tangled around arms, legs, or body

Rope neatly coiled, ready to drop in case horse bolts

Has on western boots for safety

around one hand. She may believe this will help her hold onto the horse if he tries to run away. Wrong. If a horse does bolt and run, he's so strong he'll just drag the rope and the kid along with him.

So tell your child she should never wrap the rope around her waist, hand, or any other part of her body. The horse may be gentle and well-trained. But if he gets spooked and runs, she should just drop the rope and let him go. That's also true of a pony. There's no way your kid can match her strength against a horse's mighty muscles. And she should never forget that he has a pea brain. If he's feeling ornery, she cannot make him behave.

A child who knows how to lead a big, dumb horse correctly has taken a major step toward adult responsibility. And later in life, when confronted with other bigger-than-herself challenges, she'll be more likely to take charge with confidence. It's been said that a girl who learns to handle a horse will grow up to be a woman who knows how to handle a man. But we wouldn't touch that with a ten-foot pole.

86. How to Carry a Bike

There's a right and a wrong way to do everything, and the wrong way often just makes a mess.

—Cool Mom saying

Riding his bike frees your child's spirit. He could pedal for hours, his hair ruffling in the wind. But there comes a time in every child's life when he has to pick up his bike and lift it over a fence or carry it to the car or through a park where bikes aren't allowed. And that's when trouble erupts. Bikes are cumbersome and awkward to lift. Before he's gone two steps, he's got bike-chain grease smeared all over his shirt and a sharp cog stabbing his leg.

Fortunately, you know a secret that will help your child carry his bike with Lance Armstrong flair. Have him stand to the left of the bike before picking it up. Why? Because all the messy, greasy, yucky stuff is on the right side of the bike. By standing on the left, he'll stay well away from the greasy chain and the sharp cogs of the chain wheels.

Once your kid is standing to the left of the bike, show him how to hoist it onto his shoulder. First, have him grip the handlebars with his left hand and the top tube running from the seat to the handlebars with his right hand. Second, as he lifts the wheel with his left hand, he should bend and raise his right elbow, as if he were lifting a barbell. Finally, have him swing his left shoulder under the bike and hook his right elbow over the down tube.

When the bike's properly balanced, all its weight should rest on his shoulder. His right elbow and left hand are just there to steady the bike, so it won't flip out of his hands. As he moves forward with the bike on his shoulder, have him keep the front wheel turned away from his leg, so he won't get tripped.

By showing your child the right way to carry his bike, you're teaching him to think ahead to avoid troubles. A thing done right today means less trouble tomorrow.

87. How to Ice-Skate Backward

What we call failure is not the falling down, but the staying down.
—Mary Pickford, Cool Mom of Hollywood

Ice-skating forward is a lot like walking. Any kid can do it. She just picks up her foot, steps forward, and glides. But when a kid tries moving the same way in reverse, it doesn't work. She just stands stock-still. Either that, or she does her version of the ice-skater's splits. She's mystified. How do you ice-skate backward? Those few kids who can skate backward look as if they're performing some sort of gliding magic.

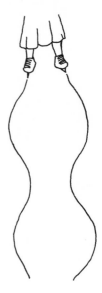

But you know what looks like magic is only a simple backward stroke called the swizzle. When a kid does the swizzle correctly, her skates will leave a tracing on the ice like that shown here. So what's the secret to doing the swizzle? Have your child bend her knees and wiggle, as if she's doing that old dance called the Twist.

1. With her knees bent (the key to balance), have your child stand pigeon-toed.

2. Now, leaning with her weight just slightly on the balls of her feet, have her push back with both feet, gliding along the inside edges of the skate blades. Remind her to sway her hips to one side as if she's doing the Twist. If she's stuck and can't move, have her bend her knees more to get started. If she hears a scratching sound as she glides backward, that's a sign she's leaning too far forward and slowing herself down with the toe picks on the front of her skates.

3. As she gains momentum—but before her knees fly apart in a split—have her swivel her heels toward each other, pulling the inside edges of her blades back together.

4. As her skates come back together, have her push off again.

Once she masters the basic swizzle, she'll then be able to go on to a full backward stroke, using the right foot, then the left foot, then the right. With practice, she'll learn how to use her arms to gain speed and how to turn. She'll begin to look like an Ice Capades star. But for now, it's enough that she can just glide backward.

By learning how to skate backward on steel blades, your child will discover the joy of mastering a skill many others can't do. But she'll also have learned to seek out answers that aren't always obvious. Later in life, when she encounters a mystifying problem at work, she may recall her ice-skating days and think, "Hold on here. Maybe there's just some important information I'm missing. Maybe I can find one hidden key that will solve the whole problem—a lot like the swizzle."

88. How to Catch a Penny off Your Elbow

We can do whatever we wish to do provided our wish is strong enough.

    —Katherine Mansfield, Cool Mom of American literature

To prove they're unique and special, kids often show off. But not knowing how to do it, they often become loud, obnoxious, and rude. So teach your child how to show off in a happy, push-back-the-envelope sort of way: Teach him how to catch a penny off his elbow.

No one knows when or where this snazzy mom skill began, but it probably dates back hundreds of years. It teaches great eye-hand coordination and the importance of concentration. First, the kid puts a penny on his elbow. Then as he suddenly drops his elbow, the penny (which should have fallen on the floor) "magically" appears in his hand. The secret is this: To catch the penny, your child has to bend his knees as he drops his elbow. Have him move his whole arm from the shoulder down, keeping his elbow fixed.

First have your child raise his arm with his elbow bent and his forearm horizontal, parallel with the floor (Fig. 1). If he's right-handed, his right hand should be palm up beside his right ear. Have him place a penny on his right elbow. Now as he suddenly drops his elbow, have him bend his knees and grab the penny with his right hand.

At first, he'll just slap the penny across the room or send it rolling under the sofa. Less persistent kids may quit, saying it's impossible. But encourage your child to keep trying. Make sure he keeps that elbow flexed while moving his arm at the shoulder only. As he bends his knees, have him drop his elbow rapidly down, so that his forearm actually drops out from under the penny. His right hand then snatches right at

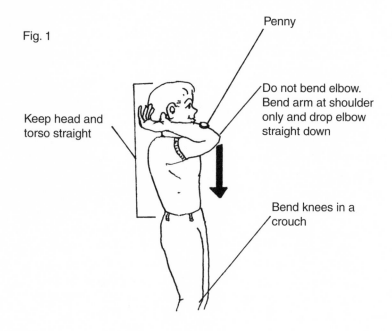

Fig. 1

Penny

Do not bend elbow. Bend arm at shoulder only and drop elbow straight down

Keep head and torso straight

Bend knees in a crouch

the space in mid-air that his elbow just vacated. With patience and concentration, he'll get it. Eventually, he'll be able to move on to two pennies, then three or four. Some whiz kids can catch twenty pennies at once.

As he learns to catch a coin off his elbow, you child will also absorb another little life lesson: Mastering any unusual skill requires sticking with it, but in the end little competencies make you feel better. Knowing you can is always better than fearing you can't.

89. How to Jump-Start a Car

Being grownup is something you decide inside yourself.
—Mary Francis Shura, Cool Mom of *The Josie Gambit*

Your sixteen-year-old recently got her driver's license. Now she's just called you at 8 P.M. from the mall. Her car won't start. She left the lights on. The battery's dead.

Is this a crisis? Not! That's because long before your kid got herself into this pickle, you taught her how to use jumper cables. The secret is this: On the top of all car batteries, you'll see two clearly-marked posts or terminals—a positive (+) one, which is usually red or orange, and a negative (−) one, which is usually black. When hooking two batteries together with jumper cables, your teen needs to connect the positive (+) terminal on her battery to the positive (+) terminal on the other guy's battery and the negative (−) terminal on her battery to his negative (−) terminal. That's the only way her car will start.

But before using the cables, she needs to make a few safety checks. The two cars should have the same battery voltage (6, 12, or 24 volts). They should not be touching each other. Everything—all ignitions, headlights, radios, blinkers—should be turned off. Both cars should also be in "park," with their handbrakes set. Warning: When handling the jumper cables, she should *never* let the red (+) clamps touch the black (−) clamps.

Now, starting with the bad battery, she should take the cables and follow these four steps:

1. Connect the first red (+) clamp on the cable to the post marked positive (+) on her dead battery.

2. Connect the other red (+) clamp to the positive (+) post on the good battery.

3. Connect one black (–) clamp to the negative (–) post on the good battery.

4. Connect the other black (–) clamp to the negative (–) post on the dead battery.

Now she should have the other guy start his car. After the other car has revved up for a minute or so, she should try to start her car. If she's lucky, it will start on the first try. If her car won't crank over but sounds as if it's about to, she should give it a few more minutes and have the other guy rev up his motor a bit. Still trouble? Have her recheck the cable connections, wait a few minutes, then try again. (If she gets a few sparks when adjusting the cables, that's normal.)

Once her car starts, she should let it run for a few minutes. Then she should disconnect the jumper cables in REVERSE order (very important), starting with step 4 above and ending with step 1. Now that she's started the car, she can come home.

A kid who can drive feels free. But one who knows how to jump-start a car is on the road to true independence.

90. How to Relieve Night Terrors

Nothing in life is to be feared. It is only to be understood.
                    —Marie Curie, Cool Mom of radium

All kids have nightmares. But some kids have a different kind of scary dream: a night terror. The kid awakens from a sound sleep, usually between 1:00 and 3:00 A.M., often with a blood-curdling scream, but sometimes just with a whimper. His eyes are wild with fright. His breathing is shallow and fast. He looks awake. Yet he acts as if he's trapped in a nightmare. Too agitated to stay in bed, he may run through the house as if he's possessed by a demon. No amount of cuddling or soothing consoles him. If left to run its course, the terror can last for thirty or more minutes.

Even most pediatricians can't tell you how to short-circuit a night terror. But here's the time-tested, age-old mom secret: As you speak to your child in a soothing voice, give him something crunchy to eat (like a crisp apple or a few saltine crackers). Within minutes, his breathing will become normal, his agitation will subside, and he'll become fully conscious. Keep feeding him the crackers or apple until you're sure he's fully awake. Soon he'll be laughing and wondering why you're in his room in the middle of the night stuffing him full of crackers. If your child repeatedly suffers night terrors (as some do when they're sick with a fever), you may want to keep a few crackers or apples as emergency rations right beside your bed.

Of course, kids are all different. If the "crunchy snack" strategy doesn't work, here's a backup plan: Gently place the child's hand under the bathroom faucet and run warm (not hot) water over it. That can also bring him around.

In this age when parenting advice has been turned over to experts, this is one of those practical mom skills that's slowly but surely being lost. So even if your child never has a night terror, pass this secret on to other Cool Moms you know.

COOL MOM FACT

What Causes Night Terrors?

What causes night terrors? Nobody's sure. But you can relax. They're not a sign of psychological problems. They don't require medication. And most kids outgrow them by the time they're teenagers, if not sooner.

Doctors do know night terrors differ from nightmares in a number of ways. First, nightmares occur during rapid-eye-movement (REM) sleep. Night terrors occur during deep levels of non-REM sleep. It's as if the kid is dreaming wide awake. Second, most kids can remember a nightmare and tell you about it. With a night terror, your kid probably won't even remember the dream. Once he's awake, it's as if the terror never happened.

91. How to Pitch a Tent

A tent pitched in the right place is like a good friend: You can trust it during stormy weather.

—Cool Mom saying

For a kid, almost nothing can wreck a camp-out adventure. A spider in her shoes only sparks curiosity. Burnt campfire potatoes become an excuse to eat more toasted marshmallows. Even rain pattering on the tent roof creates its own special music. But rain *in* the tent and drenching her to the bone . . . well, that can be a bummer.

The easy pitching instructions that come with most tents today can lull a kid into believing that once the tent's up, her troubles are over. They're not. If she pitches her tent in the wrong place and it rains, her high adventure can quickly become a soggy nightmare. Tub tents, with their floors attached to their walls, are designed to keep water out. But once water *does* get in, you're sleeping in a bathtub. So teach your child the most important secret about pitching her new tent. It's not so much *how* she pitches as *where* she pitches it that counts.

Have your child pick out a comfortably flat spot of bare ground. It's even better if she can find a mossy spot covered with soft grass or pine needles. To avoid putting undue stress on the tent floor (which could puncture it), have her clear away any rocks and sticks.

Now have your child look around and note the direction of the wind. She doesn't want to set up her tent with an open door facing the wind. If it does, the wind can blow rain into her tent during the night. She also doesn't want her doorway facing the east, where the morning sun will shine in on her.

Once your child has prepared her site, each tent has its own set of instructions telling how to set it up. Make sure she pitches the tent tautly enough so rainwater can't form puddles in the roof but not so tight that the stitching in the fabric gets stretched. Your child can use a small hammer to drive the stakes into the ground. Or, if you're in a hurry—perhaps a storm's brewing and you want to pitch the tent fast—you can have her tie the tent lines around some large rocks she's collected.

As your child learns all this, she's also learning some important lessons about foresight. She's learning to anticipate troubles and head them off. Once she's pitched the tent, most of the hard work is done. She has a secure home away from home. Now she just has to gather kindling, build a cozy campfire, and roast a few hot dogs.

92. How to Win More Points in Ping-Pong

You decide what it is you want to accomplish and then you lay out your plans to get there, and then you just do it. It's pretty straight-forward.

—Nancy Ditz, Cool Mom of Olympic running

Ping-Pong is a good game for kids. It doesn't call for long arms, broad shoulders, or fast feet. Also, the ball is small and light. Short of some freak accident, a young child will never get hurt by that tiny celluloid ball.

Does this make Ping-Pong easy? Does it require no skills at all? No way. Ping-Pong is a game of fast reflexes and great skills. And it has a secret. Your kid needs to keep the ball out of her opponent's "power zones."

What are power zones? Those are the places on the table where the other guy can reach the ball most easily with his forehand or backhand shots. He can return the ball without having to move much. When your kid hits a ball into one of these power zones, the ball can be returned with the most power and the least effort. Not good. The other guy can be lazy and still return the ball crisply. Your kid needs to make her opponent sweat for those points.

So where are these power zones she's supposed to avoid?

Fig. 1

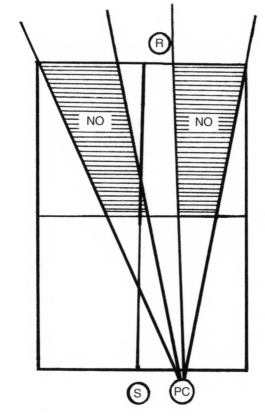

S=Server
R=Receiver
PC=Point of Contact (of the ball)

219

The forehand power zone ranges from one to three feet out from her opponent's right hip. The backhand power zone ranges from her opponent's left hip to two feet out. (See shaded areas in Fig. 1.) This holds true, no matter where her opponent moves.

Have her aim the ball for those spots on the table out of his power zones (the unshaded areas). Aiming directly down the center (between the two power zones) works especially well. The other guy has to pause for a split second to think. Should he return the ball with his forehand or backhand? Should he move left or right? Even if he manages to return the ball, he'll be off-balance for his next shot, which will work to your child's advantage.

By avoiding the receiver's power zones, your child is learning how to out-think her opponent at Ping-Pong. But she's also absorbing a deeper life lesson. As the other player keeps making wild off-balance shots and the score mounts in her favor, she'll come to realize that in Ping-Pong, as in the game of life, winning seldom results from brute strength alone. Winners usually have a powerful plan others haven't worked to develop.

93. How to Make Everybody Feel Better

Family happiness is always homemade.

—Cool Mom saying

As a Cool Mom, you're a master at cheering your kids up. Whether you're baking chocolate-chip cookies from scratch or building a fort out of an old cardboard box, you're telling your kids, "This takes extra time, but you're worth it." Still, there come moments in any mom's 24/7 life when the kids are bickering, dinner is late, the dog's barking, your nerves are frazzled, and you feel as far from *The Brady Bunch* as Peg and Al Bundy.

At times like this, you need a quick, no-hassle way to short-circuit tension and make everyone feel better. Happily, you know the secret, because it's been a Cool Mom staple for generations. It's the family hug.

No one knows the origins of this amiable custom, but it's guaranteed to make the whole family feel better. You simply call out, "Family hug time!" Then you gather in a tightly knit circle and hug each other for an entire minute or two until everyone is smiling.

The family hug teaches your child it's easier to break out of a bad mood than most people think. It only takes a little love.

This excellent mom skill also gives even a three-year-old the power to interrupt family squabbles. One day your child will be calling "Family hug! Family hug!" when *you're* feeling angry or blue.

94. How to Go Tubing on the River

A river seems a magic thing. A magic, moving, living part of the very earth itself.

—Laura Gilpin, Cool Mom of photography and writing

Every kid dreams of floating lazily down the river like Huck Finn and Jim. Whether you live near a river or are just on vacation, kids want to do more than just look at the water. They want to float in it. And you know a Cool Mom skill that will satisfy this desire:. You can turn a hot summer day into a real Huckleberry Finn adventure. You can go tubing on the river.

The first thing you and your child need, of course, are—tubes. Is there a tubing concession stand near the river? Naw, that's not cool. You have to get them at a tire shop. Most tire shops have a bunch of old truck-tire tubes lying around. They cost about five or ten dollars, but sometimes (if you're lucky), you can pick them up free. Make sure the guy who sells you the tubes checks for and patches any leaks. Then go to a gas station and inflate the tubes with an air pump.

Now you're ready to tackle the rivers of the world. If you live near a river, you may already know the best tubing spots. If you're in unknown territory, ask the locals to point out the best tubing places. For a really idyllic time, you'll want a slow, lazy, shallow river. But even a lazy river can have surprisingly deep spots. So make sure the kids wear life jackets. They should also wear old sneakers to protect their feet, just in case the bottom of the river is strewn with sharp rocks.

Once you've located an appealing stretch on the river, walk down to the water and have each kid climb into a tube, making sure the metal valve stem on the tube is pointed *down* so it won't scrape his back. His legs should hang over the tube, with his bottom dangling in the water. Get into a tube yourself, assuming this same ignoble position. Now, let nature guide you. Just float gently down the river, free as a leaf on the water.

Tell your child to watch out for rocks ahead and on the bottom (he doesn't want to scrape his shins or knees). Other than those cautions, this is one of the safest adventures on the planet. Float downstream for no longer than thirty minutes or so before you begin heading back upstream. When you're swimming against the current, even an extremely lazy river can seem relentless. As you patiently work your way back upstream, you may want to sing a "working song" as you swim, such as "I've Been Working on the Railroad," or, appropriately enough, "Old Man River." If the current is too strong to swim against or if the river is too deep for your kid to touch bottom, you'll probably want to park the car downstream, walk the road upstream, then tube back to the car.

Tubing on the river is one of life's great adventures. And as you and your kid steadily paddle your way back upstream to your starting place, he'll learn a valuable lesson: The most rewarding kinds of fun in life often involve doin' a little work.

95. How to Crack an Egg with One Hand

Nothing stimulates the practiced cook's imagination like an egg.
—Irma S. Rombauer and Marion Rombauer Becker,
the Cool Moms of *The Joy of Cooking*

To a child, cracking an egg is intriguing. Who would think such a clean white shell would contain such a sloopy, goopy mess? But most kids underestimate the strength of an egg. That white shell looks so delicate and fragile, they think the slightest tap will cause it to shatter into a trillion pieces. So they timidly *tap-tappity-tap* on the shell, and their worst fears come true. Instead of cracking the egg cleanly, they wind up with a bowlful of eggshells.

You know, however, that an egg is a lot tougher than it looks. You also know a cool way to crack an egg. Do it with one hand. The secret to success, not a mess, lies in a sharp, bold flick of the wrist.

Inside that fragile shell lies a thin but surprisingly strong membrane that holds the eggshell together. To slice crisply through that membrane and crack the shell cleanly into only two pieces, your kid just has to give the egg a quick, sharp crack of authority.

Have your child hold the egg in one hand, with her ring

finger and middle finger at the bottom of the egg and her index finger and thumb on top. Now have her give the egg a quick, sharp crack on the edge of a glass mixing bowl or measuring cup. Encourage her to be bold, confident, and authoritative. Striking the bowl too timidly will only result in a bowl specked with eggshells. Also, make sure the edge she strikes the shell against is fairly thin. Too broad an edge—such as the edge of a large metal skillet—can make the egg crumble.

As soon as the egg cracks, have your child spread her thumb and index fingers apart from her middle and ring fingers. If she's got the right touch, the shell will split completely open, and the contents will drop neatly into the bowl.

If she messes up an egg or two (or a dozen), that's OK. Even if she thinks she can't do it, tell her to keep trying. Before long, she'll be cracking eggs with the flair of Julia Child. She'll also have learned that success at egg cracking, like anything in life, requires two vital ingredients: stick-to-itiveness and enthusiasm.

96. How to Make a Daisy Chain

I am inclined to think that the flowers we most love are those we knew when we were very young, when our senses were most acute to color and to smell, and our natures most lyrical.

—Dorothy Thompson, Cool Mom of
The Courage to Be Happy

Wildflower meadows and flower gardens beckon to children like ponds beckon to ducks. One child loves to dance and run through the flowers. Another loves to loiter and bury her face in the soft, fragrant petals. But whatever your child's nature, you know a Cool Mom skill that will help her remember that wildflower field or garden forever. You know how to make a daisy chain.

Fig. 1

When most children try to make a daisy chain for the first time, they think they need to knot the stems to tie the flowers together. But you know that trying to knot delicate plant stems will only cause them to fray. To make a daisy chain correctly, your child needs to twist the stems "just so."

First have your child take two

daisies and cross the stems at right angles. Have her twist the second stem, looping it around the first one (as in Fig. 1). Now have her repeat the process until she creates a chain as long as she pleases. As a finishing touch, she can tuck in any loose strands, weaving them neatly among the other stems.

To make a necklace or bracelet, your child can simply insert the tail of the last daisy stem into loops made from the first and second daisy stems, completing the circle (Fig.2).

Making a daisy chain teaches your child to slow down and participate in the beauties of nature. And later in life, she'll be among those happy people who are never too busy to appreciate life's simple pleasures. We should all take time to stop and admire the daisies.

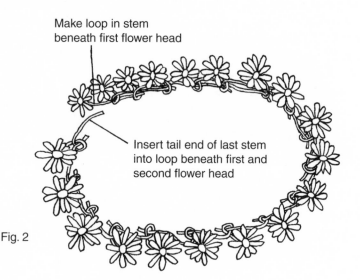

Make loop in stem beneath first flower head

Insert tail end of last stem into loop beneath first and second flower head

Fig. 2

97. How to Comfort the Cat

When my cat is feeling bad, / I sometimes talk to him. / He sits and listens all the while / Like a patient seraphim.

—Cool Mom rhyme

Cats comfort everyone around them. Nothing's more peaceful and reassuring than a cat's purr. But at times—such as when a stranger walks into the house—the cat can become agitated and worried. The pupils in his eyes get big, his ears perk up, he looks frantically around, and his tail may twitch. The cat is saying, "I'm not sure what this stranger in the house means." That's when you can teach your child to talk to the cat and say something useful. You know how your kid can use cat language to say, "Everything's OK."

The secret is this: Your child must "talk" with her eyes, not her mouth. Before she can reassure the cat, she has to get the feline's attention. Then she can use the Copasetic Blink to calm the cat down. (*Copasetic*, in case your kid asks, means "very satisfactory" or "fine and dandy.")

Tell your child to catch the cat's eye. Then while the cat is staring at her, have her blink slowly and hold her eyes closed long enough to say, "Everything's copasetic." Now have her reopen her eyes. This is exactly the signal cats use when they want to reassure and comfort each other.

The cat will probably immediately look away (a sure sign

of relaxation). Then he'll calm down. If the visitor doesn't make some surprising movement or sudden noise, the cat will begin to accept the stranger in the house as no threat.

Tell your child she can also use this silent message to reassure any cat when she's the stranger in someone else's house. It's like telling a human, in a very soothing voice, "Relax. Everything's going to be just fine."

This is also a good way to teach your child the importance of treating the cat and all other animals kindly. As stewards of the Earth, we should always go out of our way to reassure others.

98. How to Lose Like a Winner

Real courage is when you know you're licked before you begin, but you see it through no matter what.
        —Harper Lee, Cool Mom of *To Kill a Mockingbird*

Any kid can look great when he's winning—when he's flying around the bases with the wind in his hair and his team is up 12 to 1. Or when he's dribbling up the court with the score 92 to 36 in his team's favor. But what about those wretched days when your kid's team is losing—not just by a few points, but big-time? Worse, what if the other team is so dominating your child's team has almost no chance? What if they're practically beaten before they start?

Most kids in such a losing situation will whine, mope, make excuses, or even plead a bellyache before the game in an attempt to stay home. But your child comes away from a lost game with his head held high, still smiling, looking like a champion. Why? Because you've taught him a mom skill that makes him look like a winner even when he's losing. You've taught him how to forget about the score and just stay in the moment. The secret? Have him continually ask himself this question: "How can I make the best possible play *right now*?"

No one can concentrate deeply on two things at the same

time. When your child keeps his mind on the game, he stops worrying about how he looks in front of the fans. He thinks only about the fundamentals: how to hold the bat, where to place his feet, how to catch the ball. He focuses only on the joyous process of playing. He stops keeping score. In the end, because he plays so well, he may pull out a miracle. His team may actually win. But if so, that will be only a side effect of a game well-played in the moment.

A kid who knows how to do his best even in the face of defeat will come to understand the meaning of the adage that it's not winning that counts, but how you play the game. And later in life, when he's called to work against seemingly impossible odds, he'll do so without fear. He'll know that courage is a higher virtue than victory.

99. How to Write a Secret Message

A good detective is always in demand.

   —Carolyn Keene, Cool Mom of Nancy Drew mysteries

Most of a kid's life is an open book. From the hour they get up in the morning to the moment they fall asleep at night, children are being watched and told what to do. Maybe that's why they so delight in playing sleuthing games. So teach your child a secret that will sharpen her detective skills. Teach her how to write a message in invisible ink.

What's the secret? Use lemon juice. When it dries, a message written in lemon juice on white paper vanishes only to reappear when your miniature Nancy Drew and her closest pals want to read it.

First, have your child squeeze some lemon juice into a cup. Then have her dip into the juice with a small water-color brush or Q-Tip. Have her paint her "secret message" on fairly heavy white paper or a note card, then let the "ink" dry. As long as she hasn't used too much, the juice will dry clear.

Now show your child how to make the message reappear. Take the paper and hold it over a heat source—a large 150- to 200-watt electric light bulb, a toaster that's toasting bread, or for the spookiest effect, a candle flame. (Don't let the candle set the paper on fire!) The heat will turn the lemon juice a dark brown, so the message can be easily read.

Learning to make invisible ink can sharpen a child's curiosity and make her more wide-awake and keenly alert to hidden details. If a message can be invisible, what else is true, but not readily apparent? In her quest for truth, knowledge, or information, she'll be more inclined to ask questions.

COOL MOM TIP

More Invisible Inks

If you're fresh out of lemon juice, ordinary milk also makes an excellent, heat-sensitive invisible ink, as do orange juice, grapefruit juice, and white vinegar.

What makes these "inks" turn brown when they're heated? They all contain carbon compounds like those in caramel. When your child heats a sheet of paper on which an invisible message was written, the carbon gets scorched. It's the same sort of reaction that occurs when you burn a pie or a cookie.

---

100. How to Make Emergency Cookies

No man can be wise on an empty stomach.
                    —George Eliot, Cool Mom of many novels

Your kid is a lot like the Cookie Monster. Homemade cookies! Mmmmm, yum! Need cookies! He has no idea you've been so rushed this past week you haven't had time to get to the supermarket. The ordinary essentials for home-baked cookies—eggs, milk, chocolate chips, nuts, even frozen cookie dough—are nowhere in sight. You don't even have a whole cup of sugar.

Is this a problem? No! As any mom knows, an empty pantry is the mother of innovation. You know one recipe for real homemade cookies that requires almost no ingredients at all. It's the recipe for Scottish Shortbread. What's more, it's so simple, most kids can whip up a batch for themselves. And it's delicious! Mmmmm!

This classic cookie must have originally been dubbed "shortbread" because it's the only cookie you can bake when you're short of almost every ingredient in the pantry. Yet it's so delicious it will satisfy the most voracious cookie monster's sweet tooth. Here's the emergency recipe to share with your child, so he can make cookies for himself when the larder is almost bare:

- ⅔ cup (that's one stick plus three tablespoons) of butter or margarine, at room temperature (in a pinch, a solid shortening like Crisco will also work)
- ½ cup granulated sugar (powdered sugar will also do)
- ½ cup plus 2 tablespoons all-purpose flour (white is best, but brown's OK)
- ½ teaspoon salt.

Preheat the oven to 325 degrees. Cream the butter or margarine in a bowl. Gradually add the sugar, and beat until fluffy with a small mixer. Toss in the flour and salt. Then have your child scrunch all the ingredients together with his bare hands. The butter and flour mixtures should be thoroughly blended.

Press the dough into a nine-inch pie pan. Pinch the edges of the dough to form a pretty rim. Prick the dough about twelve times with a fork. Using a sharp knife, mark the dough into sixteen wedges, cutting about halfway through each wedge.

Bake the dough until it is very lightly browned on the edges only, about 50 minutes. When the cookies are done, the center still won't be brown. But the center will feel firm when pressed gently. Remove the cookies from the oven and cool them in the pan. Cut the cookies along the marked wedges and devour.

With this handy emergency recipe in his arsenal, your cookie monster will never know how close he came to cookie deprivation. At the same time, he'll have learned how to fend for himself. Making his own shortbread is one small step toward culinary independence.

101. How to Blow a Six-Foot (or Bigger) Soap Bubble

Nothing is impossible; we just don't know how to do it yet.
—L. L. Larison Cudmore, Cool Mom of cell biology

Nothing's more enchanting than a rainbow-hued soap bubble dancing on air. And no one's more delighted than the child who can blow one. But there is a way you can lead your child to a bigger adventure that will knock her socks off and wow all her friends. Teach her the secret of blowing a six-foot soap bubble—or bigger.

Of all the secrets required to blow gargantuan bubbles, the most important is this: The air has to be humid. You can't swim without water or fly a kite without wind, and you can't blow a six-foot soap bubble without high humidity. On a cool summer day right after a rain or on a foggy day near the sea, that's when big bubbles flourish, float, and don't instantly pop. Your child should also avoid too much wind. OK, that's the secret. Now here's the plan.

Other than high humidity, your kid needs two things to blow a soap bubble the size of a small car: a long piece of loosely woven, inch-wide fabric trim and the right soap formula (very important). Liquid Joy Ultra is by far the best big-

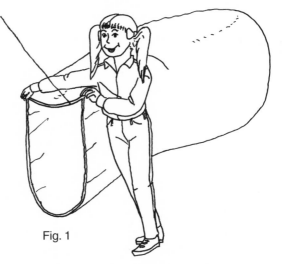

This part of the loop holds the extra bubble solution for making big bubbles. To make larger bubbles get it as full as possible.

Fig. 1

bubble soap, although some bubble masters insist green (not blue, not orange) Dawn also works well. Add two cups of Joy to a small bucket containing six cups of cold, clean water and ¾ cup of white Karo syrup. Mix the solution a bit with your hand, but don't create a lot of foam, or big bubbles won't form. To work best, let stand for twenty-four hours.

Now here's how your child can invent his own Super Bubble Blower:

1. Take a piece of loosely woven fabric trim about an inch wide and seven feet long. Tie the two ends together to form a complete loop.

2. When she picks up the loop, she should leave a short piece of fabric trim (about two feet) dangling between her hands (Fig. 1). This will be the top part of the loop. The more soap solution she has in this part of the loop, the bigger her bubble will be.

3. Holding her hands together, she should dip the whole loop in and out of the solution. Make sure no part of the loop beomes twisted.

4. Now as she walks or turns gently (to create a small breeze), she should carefully spread her hands and open the loop.

5. The bubble will form behind her, streaming out of the loop (Fig. 1). Now she should gently bring the fabric trim back together to close off the bubble.

6. Between bubbles, run thumb and forefinger down the fabric trim to get rid of froth buildup. She can also keep a bucket of clean water or a garden hose handy to rinse the froth off between bubbles.

At first, she may not get a full bubble. Super-colossal bubbles are tricky. If she has troubles, go back over the basics: the right formula, no froth, high humidity, not too much wind. On a low-humidity day, she may need to add more water to her solution. This is a science. It takes some experimenting. Once some bubbles are half forming, she's almost got it. With enough patience, perseverance, and experimentation, she'll get it. And when she does, she'll create the most *supercalifragilisticexpialidocious* bubble ever! Because this is a tricky skill to master, she'll also be the only kid in the neighborhood who can do it.

Which just goes to show, if you want to be a cool kid, it helps to have a Cool Mom.